WISH LIST

by Katherine Soper

24 September–15 October 2016
Royal Exchange Theatre, Manchester

10 January–11 February 2017
Royal Court Theatre, London

The first performance of *Wish List* was at the
Royal Exchange Theatre on 24 September 2016

WISH LIST

by Katherine Soper

CAST

TAMSIN CARMODY	Erin Doherty
DEAN CARMODY	Joseph Quinn
THE LEAD	Aleksandar Mikic
LUKE MBURU	Shaquille Ali-Yebuah

CREATIVE TEAM

DIRECTOR	Matthew Xia
DESIGNER	Ana Inés Jabares-Pita
LIGHTING DESIGNER	Ciarán Cunningham
COMPOSER & SOUND DESIGNER	Giles Thomas
CASTING DIRECTOR	Sophie Parrott CDG
MOVEMENT DIRECTOR	Angela Gasparetto
ASSISTANT DIRECTOR	Monique Touko
STAGE MANAGER	Lynsey Fraser
DEPUTY STAGE MANAGER	Caoimhe Regan

Monique Touko Three-Month Placement at Royal Exchange Theatre through Regional Theatre Young Director Scheme

THE COMPANY

ERIN DOHERTY (Tamsin Carmody) trained at Bristol Old Vic Theatre school and is making her first appearance for the Royal Exchange Theatre. Previous theatre credits include: *The Glass Menagerie* (UK tour); *Pink Mist* (Bristol Old Vic) and *Peter O'Toole Memorial* (Old Vic). Credits in training include: *The Grand Gesture, The Heresy of Love, The Comedy of Errors, The Last Days of Judas Iscariot, Twelfth Night, Uncle Vanya* and *Speaking in Tongues.*

JOSEPH QUINN (Dean Carmody) trained at LAMDA and is making his first appearance for the Royal Exchange Theatre. Previous theatre credits include: *Deathwatch* (Print Room). Credits in training include: *Henry IV Part 1, The English Game, Titus Andronicus, The Seagull* and *The Changeling.* Television credits include: *Dickensian* and *Postcode.*

ALEKSANDAR MIKIC (The Lead) is making his first appearance at the Royal Exchange Theatre. Previous theatre credits include: *Suddenly Last Summer* and *The Cherry Orchard* (Citizens Theatre); *Guilt* (7:84 Theatre Company); *Cruel and Tender* (Young Vic); *King Lear, The Government Inspector* and *5/11* (Chichester Festival Theatre); *Petrol Jesus Nightmare No.5* (Traverse); *The Reporter* (National Theatre); *Truth and Reconciliation* (Royal Court). Television credits include: *Doctor Who, Spooks, Messiah, Prime Suspect, The Comic Strip Presents, Hope Springs, EastEnders, Not Going Out, Last Detective, Blue Murder, Hotel Babylon, Belle de Jour, Gunrush, The Fixer, Trial and Retribution, Prisoners' Wives, Lucan* and *The Gates.* Film credits include: *Extraordinary Rendition, Eastern Promises, It's a Free World, The Sweeney, Red 2, Tarzan* and *Black Forrest.*

SHAQUILLE ALI-YEBUAH (Luke Mburu) is making his first appearance for the Royal Exchange Theatre. Television credits include: *Dixi, You, Me & the Apocalypse, In & Out of the Kitchen, Tag* and *Casualty.* Film credits include: *iBoy, Social Suicide, Legacy, What Comes After, Some Things Mean Something, I Only Have Eyes For You* and *Year 7.*

KATHERINE SOPER (Writer) studied playwriting at Royal Central School of Speech and Drama, where she wrote *Wish List.* She also wrote *Star Jelly* for the 2016 RHS Flower Show at Tatton Park. She has developed work with a Studio Group at the Royal Court and with the Young Friends of the Almeida.

MATTHEW XIA (Director) is Associate Artistic Director at the Royal Exchange Theatre. He was previously Director in Residence at the Liverpool Everyman & Playhouse and Associate Director at Theatre Royal Stratford East. Directing credits for the Royal Exchange include: *Into the Woods* and *Brink*. Other directing credits include: *Blue/Orange*, *Sizwe Banzi is Dead* and *The Sound of Yellow* (Young Vic); *Migration Music* and *Scrappers* (Liverpool Everyman); *When Chaplin Met Gandhi* (Kingsley Hall); *The Blacks*, *Cinderella* and *I Was Looking at the Ceiling and Then I Saw the Sky* (Co-Director, Theatre Royal Stratford East); *Soundbites: Ruth The Divorcee and Barry the Love-Sick Bee* (Lyric Theatre Studio/Bestival); *Wild Child* (Royal Court Jerwood Theatre Upstairs); *Re:Definition* (Hackney Empire); *Mad Blud* and *Aladdin* (Associate Director, Theatre Royal Stratford East) and *In His Hands* (Urban Theatre). Assistant director credits include: *The Misanthrope* (Liverpool Everyman) and *Blackta* (Young Vic). Composing/sound design credits: Paralympics Opening Ceremony (DJ); *That's The Way To Do It* (Time Won't Wait); *Squid* (Theatre Royal Stratford East); *Free Run* (Underbelly); *Bolero Remixed* and *Pass the Baton* (New London Orchestra).

ANA INÉS JABARES-PITA (Designer) has earned two stage design awards. The first one came in 2013 for her design for *Sappho... In 9 Fragments,* Best Set Design Award at the Fringe Theatre Festival in Ottawa. The second one was also in 2013, when she won the most prestigious UK Stage Design Award for emerging designers, The Linbury Prize. She was announced as the overall winner for her design proposal of *The Driver's Seat* for the National Theatre of Scotland, which premiered in 2015 to great reviews – on this occasion Ana Inés designed set, costume and video. Her work crosses a range of genres: opera, ballet, theatre, installation and film. She also has an extensive grounding in music which made her become interested in sound as part of scenography. In 2014 she became part of the Gate Theatre's Jerwood Young Designers. Her work *Idomeneus* (Gate) has been selected by the Victoria and Albert Museum in London, to become part of their archive. It was also chosen as one of the ten best theatre productions of 2014 by Lyn Gardner (*Guardian*). Her work for *Domestica* (Sleepwalk Collective) and *Sappho... In 9 Fragments* represented Spain in the Prague Quadrennial of Scenography 2015. Some of her most recent work includes: *The Echo Chamber* (Young Vic); *Lela & Co.* (Royal Court) selected by the *Guardian* and *Huffington Post* as one of the Top 10 Theatre Productions of 2015 in the UK; *Another Love* (winner of Best International Short Film in more than three festivals and among the official selection of Cannes Film Festival). Recently she has received the Spirit of Dundee Award for her costume design, *Ignis,* at Dundee Weareable Art Competition. She has been selected in the Design category to represent Spanish Talent in the campaign 'Hechos de Talento' in more than fifteen countries all over the world.

CIARÁN CUNNINGHAM (Lighting Designer) trained at East15 Acting School where he gained a BA Honours in Stage Management and Technical Theatre (Lighting Design). Now working as a freelance lighting designer creating lighting designs for dance, theatre and music, he is also the resident Lighting Technician at The Actors Church, Covent Garden and The Tabernacle, Notting Hill. Lighting design credits for the Royal Exchange Theatre include: *Into the Woods* and *Brink.* Other lighting design credits include: *Sizwe Banzi is Dead* (Young Vic/UK tour); *Sound of Yellow* (Young Vic); *Sense of Sound's: Migration Music* (Liverpool Everyman); *Scrappers* (Liverpool Playhouse); *In His Hands; Re:Definition* and *Collision* (Hackney Empire); *A Dream Cross the Ocean* (Fairfield Hall Ashcroft Theatre); *When Chaplin Met Gandhi* (Kingsley Hall); *Oliver Twist* (Lion and Unicorn); *Chris Dugdale: 2 Face Deception* (Leicester Square); *Letter to Larry* (Jermyn Street) and *The Flouers O'Edinburgh* (Finborough). Lighting design credits for ballet and dance: *AFD: Jazz* (Florence Fould Hall NYC); *AFD: Just Dance* (Piazza Teatru Rjal Malta/Winchester Theatre Royal); *AFD: Pop 8* (Lion and Unicorn); *Up & Over It* (Hackney Empire); *Ecdysis* (Sadler's Wells Lilian Baylis Studio/UK tour); *Orixas* (The Place Robin Howard Dance Theatre/UK tour): *Evol* (Birmingham Hippodrome/ UK tour); Ladylike (Richmix/UK tour); *4 By 6* and *Realpoltik* (Michaelis) and *Birds* (UK tour).

GILES THOMAS (Composer & Sound Designer) has worked on *Yen* (also Royal Court) and *Pomona* (also National Theatre and Orange Tree) for the Royal Exchange. Other composition and sound design credits include: *Contractions* (Sheffield Theatres); *I See You* (Royal Court); *Correspondence, Sparks* (Old Red Lion); *The Titanic Orchestra, This Will End Badly, Allie* (Edinburgh); *Little Malcolm and His Struggle Against the Eunuchs* (Southwark Playhouse); *Outside Mullingar* (Theatre Royal Bath); *Back Down* (Birmingham Rep); *The Wolf from the Door, Primetime, Mint, Pigeons, Death Tax, The President Has Come To See You* (Royal Court); *Lie With Me* (Talawa); *The Sound of Yellow* (Young Vic); *Take a Deep Breath and Breathe, The Street* (Ovalhouse); *Stop Kiss* (Leicester Square). Sound design credits include: *They Drink It In The Congo* (Almeida); *The Sugar-Coated Bullets of the Bourgeoisie* (Arcola/HighTide Festival); *Decades* (The Brit School For Performing Arts); *The Snow Queen* (Southampton Nuffield/Northampton Royal & Derngate); *Orson's Shadow* (Southwark Playhouse); *Defect* (Arts Ed); *Betrayal* (I Fagiolini/UK tour);

A Harlem Dream (Young Vic); *Khandan* (Birmingham Rep/Royal Court); *Superior Donuts* (Southwark Playhouse); *Three Men in a Boat* (Original Theatre Company, UK tour); *King John* (Union); *It's About Time* (nabokov/ Hampstead); *Shoot/Get Treasure/Repeat* (Royal Court/Gate/Out of Joint/Paines Plough/National Theatre); *House of Agnes* (Paines Plough). Associate Sound Designer on: *Ma Rainey's Black Bottom* (National Theatre); *Henry IV* (Donmar Warehouse/tour); *Henry V* (Michael Grandage Company, West End); *1984* (West End/UK tour). Music Producer on: *An Appointment with the Wickerman* (National Theatre of Scotland). Screen credits include: *Aurelia* (Jade Edwards); *Ident* (Anaya Productions); Cern Hadron Collider Exhibition (Science Museum); *Street Spirit* (Tom Bailey); *Last of the Oaks* (Luis Baron). Giles was nominated for Best Sound Designer (Offie Awards 2015) for his work on *Pomona*.

SOPHIE PARROTT CDG (Casting Director) as Casting Director theatre credits include: *My Mother Said I Never Should* (St James); *Britannia Waves the Rules* (Royal Exchange, Manchester/tour); *Pomona* (additional casting for National Theatre Shed/Royal Exchange, Manchester); *Yen* (Royal Court, London/Royal Exchange, Manchester, *A Midsummer Night's Dream* (Liverpool Everyman); *The Crocodile* (Manchester International Festival); *Billy Liar* (Royal Exchange, Manchester); *Next Fall* (Southwark Playhouse); *Tutto Bene, Mamma?* (The Print Room); *Glasshouse* (Cardboard Citizens). Television includes (as Casting Director): *Doctors*; (as Casting Associate): *Rillington Place*, *Thirteen*, *Call the Midwife* series iv and v, *The Bletchley Circle II*, *Silent Witness* xvii and xviii; (as Casting Assistant): *The Game*, *Esio Trot*, *Mr Stink*, *WPC56*, *The Preston Passion*, *The Night Watch*, *Holby City*, *The Riots: In Their Own Words*, *Undeniable*. Film includes: *The Secret Agent*, *Whirlpool*, *A Street Cat Named Bob* (as Casting Associate).

ANGELA GASPARETTO (Movement Director) previous movement direction credits include: *Redefining Juliet* (BBC4); *Sizwe Banzi is Dead* (Young Vic/UK tour); *See Bob Run* (Bread & Roses); *Choir* (Encounter); *Love is Easy* (McFly video); *The Kitchen* (Fourth Monkey); *A Midsummer Night's Dream* (Custom/Practice); *Faith, Hope & Charity* (Southwark Playhouse); *Fair Trade* (Shatterbox & Emma Thompson); *The Prisoner of Zenda* (Chalkfoot Theatre Arts); *Monteverdi's Flying Circus* (Armonico Consort). Angela is resident movement director for Pied Piper Theatre Company. Direction credits include: *Life on Wheels* (Bella Kinetica); *Jon Udry Punches Gravity In The Face*, *Rapunzel* (Fourth Monkey). Angela is Course Director of Fourth Monkey's Two Year Rep Actor Training Programme and teaches at RADA.

Situated in the heart of Manchester, the Royal Exchange Theatre is one of the UK's leading producing theatres, and in January was named Regional Theatre of the Year 2016. Our ambitious programme is inspired by the world's greatest stories: stories that have the power to change the way we see the world. That means taking artistic risks, working as part of exciting partnerships, championing new talent and seeking out bold collaborations, broadening our output on and offstage, and speaking to the most diverse audiences in Manchester and beyond.

This September marks our 40th year as a Company and alongside our productions we will be presenting a programme of 40th events to celebrate the past and look forward to the future.

The Royal Exchange is committed to supporting and developing new writing. The Bruntwood Prize for Playwriting in partnership with the Royal Exchange Theatre is the UK's biggest playwriting competition and celebrated its 10th anniversary last year when the 2015 Prize was awarded to Katherine Soper for her play *Wish List*. The Bruntwood Prize for Playwriting 2017 will be launched in January 2017.

To find out more please visit royalexchange.co.uk, or follow us twitter.com/rxtheatre
facebook: royalexchangetheatre
Box Office 0161 833 9833

Registered Charity Number 255424

ROYAL EXCHANGE THEATRE STAFF

Box Office Manager
Sue Partington
Box Office Assistants
William Barnett, Jon Brennan, Lindsay Burke, Dan Glynn, Zoe Nicholas, Christine Simpson, Eleanor Walk
CASTING
Casting Director & Associate Director
Jerry Knight-Smith CDG
CATERING
General Manager
Ellen O'Donnell
Bars Manager
Chris Wilson
Hospitality Manager
Claire Molineux Jones
Supervisor Mark Beattie
Supervisor Vicky Bowen
Supervisor Jake Tysome
Head Chef
Chris Watson Gunby
Catering Team
Chris Gray, Paul Roberts, Damien Traczyk, Claudiu Codreanu
Front of House Team
Scott Folds, Sarah Hope, Paul Callaghan, Henrietta Dunn, Holly Williams, Helen Thomason, Jose Garia Carrasco, Simon Mayne, Cat Belcher, Hannah Sian Jones, Emma Gold, Harry Egan, Elena Bernal Rodriguez, Leah Curran, Robin Lyons
COMPANY
Company Manager
Lee Drinkwater
COSTUME HIRE
Costume Hire Manager Ludmila Krzak
With help from volunteer team
CRAFT SHOP
Manager Rachael Noone
Deputy Manager
Gail Owen
Assistants Anne Kelsall, Elisa Robertson, Amber Samuels, Clare Sidebotham, Emily Tilzey
DEVELOPMENT
Development Director
Val Young
Senior Development Manager Gina Fletcher
Development Manager Becky Rosenthal
Development Manager
Christina Georgiou
Development Executive Holli Leah
Membership Manager
Jessica Hilton
DIRECTORATE
Executive Director
Mark Dobson

Artistic Director
Sarah Frankcom
Associate Artistic Director Matthew Xia
Associate Artists
Maxine Peake, Benji Reid, Chris Thorpe
Director of Engagement
Amanda Dalton
Senior Producer
Richard Morgan
Producer Amy Clewes
Assistant to the Artistic Directorate & Executive Director
Michelle Hickman
Birkbeck Trainee Director Andy Routledge
FINANCE & ADMINISTRATION
Director of Finance & Administration
Barry James
HR Manager
Yvonne Cox
Finance Manager
Sue Jones
Orders & Purchase Ledger Clerk
Jennifer Ellis
Payroll Clerk
Carl Robson
GREEN ROOM
Supervisor Yvonne Stott
Assistant Anne Dardis
INFORMATION TECHNOLOGY
IT Manager Ean Burgon
IT Support & Network Technician Zak Clifford
LITERARY
New Writing Associate
Suzanne Bell
Literary Department & Talent Development Administrator
Davinia Jokhi
Channel 4 Playwright
Kellie Smith
2015 Bruntwood Prize for Playwriting Playwright in Residence
Katherine Soper
Talawa Playwrights Scheme Playwright in Residence
David Judge
Revolution Mix (Eclipse Theatre Company) Playwright in Residence Afshan Lodhi
Kenyon Playwrights Commission
Charlene James
LIGHTING
Head of Lighting
Mark Distin-Webster
Senior Technicians
Alex Dixon, Matt Lever

Technician
Louise Anderson
MARKETING
Director of Marketing
Claire Will
Head of Marketing
Vanessa Walters
Design & Print Manager Maxine Laing
Communications Manager Paula Rabbitt
Marketing Officer – Digital & Systems
Caspar Stevens
Marketing Officer – Groups, Education & Development
Eleanor Higgins
Marketing Officer
Anneka Morley
Marketing Assistant
Ashley McKay
Archivist (Volunteer)
Stella Lowe
PARTICIPATION & LEARNING
Head of Participation and Learning
Sarah Lovell
Producer – Creative Industry Experience
Chris Wright
Adults Programme Leader Andy Barry
Community Programme Leader
Tracie Daly
Schools Programme Leader Chelsea Morgan
Young People's Programme Leader
Matt Hassall
Administrator
Emma Wallace
Participation and Learning Admin Assistant Allan Foy
PRODUCTION
Head of Production
Simon Curtis
Head of Technical Production
Richard Delight
Production Co-ordinator
Greg Skipworth
Props Buyer Kim Ford
Driver John Fisher
PROPS & SETTINGS
Head of Props & Settings Neil Gidley
Deputy Head of Props & Settings
Andrew Bubble
Senior Scenic Artist
Philip Costello
Prop Makers Ben Cook, Carl Heston, Stuart Mitchell, Meriel Pym, Sarah Worrall

SOUND
Head of Sound
Sorcha Williams
Senior Technician
David Norton
Technician
Matthew Masson
STAGE
Technical Stage Manager Andy Roberts
Technicians Luke Murray, Simon Wild
VISITOR EXPERIENCE
Operations Director
Jo Topping
Visitor Experience Manager Lynne Yates
Deputy Visitor Experience Manager
Stuart Galligan
Facilities Manager
David Mitchell
Hire & Events Assistant Allan Foy
Relief FOH Managers
Jill Bridgman, Rachel Davies
Relief Deputy Managers Helen Coyne, Chris Dance, Dan Glynn
Security Liam Ainsworth, Liam Carty, David Hughes, Mike Seal
Stage Door Thomas Flaherty, Peter Mainka
Head Cleaner
Lillian Williams
Cleaners Vera Asara, Gillian Bradshaw, Susan Burrough, Elaine Connolly, Valarie Daffern, Jackie Farnell, Ahab Mohamed, Maryam Murmin, Daniel Thompson
Ushers Liam Ainsworth, Tom Banks, Jill Bridgman, Georgie Brown, Helen Brown, Sarah Button, Natasha Bybik, Elizabeth Callan,Liam Carty, Emily Chadwick, Richard Challinore, Alicia Cole, Liz Coupe, Helen Coyne, Chris Dance, Anna Davenport, Rachel Davies, Luther Edmead, Paul Evans, Neil Fenton, Tracey Fleet, Beth Galligan, Dan Glynn, Tyler Gorden, Jamie Leigh Hargreaves, Connie Hartley, Sarah Hill, Jen Hulman, Dan Lizar, Ben Lucas, Heather Madden, Susan Mcgonnell, Tony O'Driscoll, Annie Roberts, John Roy, Mike Seal, Eleanor Theodorou, Vincent Tuohy, Ted Walker, Judith Wood, Mahdi Zadeh

DONORS, SUPPORTERS AND BENEFACTORS

PRINCIPAL FUNDERS

MAJOR SPONSORS

manchester airport

CHEETHAM BELL

PROJECT SUPPORTERS

Addleshaw Goddard
The Andrew Lloyd
   Webber Foundation
The Beaverbrooks
   Charitable Trust
Arnold & Brenda
Bradshaw
The Co-operative
   Foundation
Computeam
Duchy of Lancaster
Benevolent Fund
Esmèe Fairbairn Foundation
Garfield Weston
Foundation
The Granada Foundation
Equity Charitable Trust –
The John Fernald Award
The J Paul Getty Jnr
   Charitable Trust
The John Thaw Foundation
King Street Townhouse
   Hotel
The Madeleine Mabey
   Trust
Manchester Guardian
   Society
The Noël Coward
   Foundation
The Oglesby Charitable
   Trust
The Paul Hamlyn
   Foundation
The Peter Henriques
   Memorial Fund
The PWC Foundation
The Raffle family
The Rayne Foundation
The Rycroft Children's Fund
Schroder Charitable Trust

Susan Hodgkiss CBE
Martyn & Valerie Torevell
We are AD

PRINCIPAL MEMBERSHIP

Bruntwood
Cheetham Bell
Edmundson Electrical
Havas Lynx
Neil Eckersley Productions
Regatta

ENCORE MEMBERSHIP

Beaverbrooks
Dewhurst Torevell
M.A.C Cosmetics

ASSOCIATE MEMBERSHIP

Acies Group
Addleshaw Goddard
Cityco
Computeam
Galloways Printers
Grant Thornton
HFL Building Solutions
Hollins Strategic Land
King Street Townhouse
Hotel
Mills & Reeve
Pinsent Masons
RSM
Sanderson Weatherall
Sapphire Systems
Smart Alex
Whitebirk Finance Ltd

PATRONS £1000+ PA

Arnold & Brenda
   Bradshaw
Ben & Maggie Caldwell
Maureen Casket
Meg Cooper
Barbara Crossley
Brendan & Ellen Flood
The Harrison Family
Nick & Lesley Hopkinson
Richard & Elaine Johnson
William & Ariel Lees-Jones
Sandy Lindsay
Stuart Montgomery
Christine Ovens
Stephen & Judy Poster
UK Together
& all our anonymous
patrons

PLATINUM MEMBERSHIP

Chris & Sue Bangs
Mr J Bishop & Mr J Taylor
Angela Brookes
Professor R A Burchell
John & Penny Early

Peter & Judy Folkman
Samantha Rollason
Martin & Sandra Stone
Robin & Mary Taylor
Helen & Phil Wiles

CATALYST DONORS

Anonymous
Roy Beckett
Sir Robert &
   Mrs Meriel Boyd
Bernard & Julie De Sousa
John & Penny Early
The Friends
Martin Harrison & Frances
   Hendrix
Eve & Peter Keeling
Chris & Mike Potter
Dr J L Pearsall
Jennifer Raffle
Martyn & Valerie Torevell
Gerry & Joanne Yeung

REGULAR GIVING MEMBERS

Gold Membership
£240+pa
G W Ball
Gary Buttriss-Holt
Ronald Cassidy
Mr Peter Cooper
Mr P J Craven
Mrs Valerie Dunne
Rosalind Emsley-Smith
Mrs V Fletcher
James Garbett
Irene Gray
Mrs L Hawkins
George Ian Hood
Patricia Rose Kelly
Gillian & Kieron Lonergan
Sheila Malone
Jon Mason
Mr Donald Mather
Mr & Mrs Meldrum
Mr G M Morton
Pannone LLP
Mrs Maria Price
Mr & Mrs Rose
Sandra Thomas
Mr J D Wignall

For a full list of Silver
Membership
supporters please visit
royalexchange.co.uk
/donors For more
information on how you
can support the work of the
Royal Exchange Theatre
please contact the
Development Department
on 0161 615 6759

THE ROYAL COURT THEATRE

The Royal Court Theatre is the writers' theatre. It is the leading force in world theatre for energetically cultivating writers – undiscovered, emerging and established.

Through the writers, the Royal Court is at the forefront of creating restless, alert, provocative theatre about now. We open our doors to the unheard voices and free thinkers that, through their writing, change our way of seeing.

Over 120,000 people visit the Royal Court in Sloane Square, London, each year and many thousands more see our work elsewhere through transfers to the West End and New York, UK and international tours, digital platforms, our residencies across London, and our site-specific work. Through all our work we strive to inspire audiences and influence future writers with radical thinking and provocative discussion.

The Royal Court's extensive development activity encompasses a diverse range of writers and artists and includes an ongoing programme of writers' attachments, readings, workshops and playwriting groups. Twenty years of the International Department's pioneering work around the world means the Royal Court has relationships with writers on every continent.

Within the past sixty years, John Osborne, Samuel Beckett, Arnold Wesker, Ann Jellicoe, Howard Brenton and David Hare have started their careers at the Court.

Many others including Caryl Churchill, Athol Fugard, Mark Ravenhill, Simon Stephens, debbie tucker green, Sarah Kane - and, more recently, Lucy Kirkwood, Nick Payne, Penelope Skinner and Alistair McDowall - have followed.

The Royal Court has produced many iconic plays from Laura Wade's **Posh** to Jez Butterworth's **Jerusalem** and Martin McDonagh's **Hangmen**.

Royal Court plays from every decade are now performed on stage and taught in classrooms and universities across the globe.

www.royalcourttheatre.com

Supported using public funding by
**ARTS COUNCIL
ENGLAND**

ROYAL COURT SUPPORTERS

The Royal Court is a registered charity and not-for-profit company. We need to raise £1.7 million every year in addition to our core grant from the Arts Council and our ticket income to achieve what we do.

We have significant and longstanding relationships with many generous organisations and individuals who provide vital support. Royal Court supporters enable us to remain the writers' theatre, find stories from everywhere and create theatre for everyone.

We can't do it without you.

Supported using public funding by
ARTS COUNCIL ENGLAND

The Royal Court has been on the cutting edge of new drama for nearly 60 years. Thanks to our members, we are able to undertake the vital support of writers and the development of their plays – work which is the lifeblood of the theatre.

In acknowledgement of their support, members are invited to venture beyond the stage door to share in the energy and creativity of Royal Court productions.

Please join us as a member to celebrate our shared ambition whilst helping to ensure our ongoing success.

We can't do it without you.
royalcourttheatre.com

BECOME A MEMBER

To join as a Royal Court member from £250 a year, please contact

Charlotte Cole, Development Officer
charlottecole@royalcourttheatre.com
020 7565 5049

The English Stage Company at the Royal Court Theatre is a registered charity (No. 231242).

LOVE
NEW
WRITING

"It is easy to lose faith in an over subscribed industry that has very little funding to support new work, but the Bruntwood Prize is that opportunity. It changed my life."

Gareth Farr
Judges Prize winner of The Bruntwood Prize for Playwriting 2011
for his play *Britannia Waves The Rules*

The 2017 Bruntwood Prize for Playwriting launching January 2017.

Over our 40-year history as one of Manchester's largest property companies, Bruntwood has always played an active part in the city and its community.

We are family owned and run, and have a strong belief that what is good for the cities we operate in is good for our customers and good for our business. That's why we are committed to pledging 10% of our annual profits to supporting the arts and other charitable and environmental activities.

bruntwood

For more information visit:
bruntwood.co.uk/the-bruntwood-way

WISH LIST

Katherine Soper

Acknowledgements

Enormous thanks must go to everyone at the Royal Exchange, Bruntwood, and the readers, administrators, and judges of the Bruntwood Prize. Thank you for seeing something in my work.

Thanks also to:

Melissa Dunne. Davina Moss. Salome Wagaine. Everyone at Central, especially Sarah Grochala for suggesting I write this idea instead of my other one. The staff of the much-missed Nomad Books café, where the 2014 version was written. Every single member of my extended Penhaligon's family. Citizens Advice and Turn2us for their tireless work and resources. The Howe family. Iliyana Todorova and Lulu Raczka for so much writerly support and reassurance. Nick Hern Books. Jonathan Kinnersley. The brilliant actors who helped workshop the script: Katie West, Jamie Samuel, Ivanno Jeremiah, and Michael Peavoy. The equally brilliant actors who made the play happen: Erin Doherty, Joseph Quinn, Shaquille Ali-Yebuah, and Aleksandar Mikic.

The wonderful Matthew Xia and Suzanne Bell.

Phil, who read this more times than was probably healthy.

Finally, thanks to my parents, and to my brother.

K.S.

'From the gods who sit in grandeur
grace comes somehow violent.'

Aeschylus

Characters

DEAN CARMODY, *seventeen*
TAMSIN CARMODY, *nineteen*
THE LEAD, *thirty-eight*
LUKE MBURU, *sixteen*

Note on Play

The staging of this play is open to interpretation – the stage
directions are intended to evoke the literal world of the
characters, but do not demand a literal staging.

*This text went to press before the end of rehearsals and so may
differ slightly from the play as performed.*

Scene One

A flat in Oldbrook, Milton Keynes. August.

DEAN *is in the bathroom, applying gel to his hair. He does it very precisely and meticulously, applying far more than an average amount and twisting his hair into spikes. It should not be a hairstyle that seems familiar or attractive.*

TAMSIN *knocks on the door, deliberately gently.*

TAMSIN. Hey.

Sorry about earlier.

Do you want any help?

I'm just gonna be in my room, so let me know.

She retreats to her own room.

The loud ringing of a phone on the top of the loo startles DEAN, and breaks his concentration. He looks at it as though it might attack him. He breathes in and out a few times.

He gingerly picks it up and tries, mentally, to prepare himself to answer, but puts it back down almost the moment he lifts it to his ear.

He returns to the sink.

TAMSIN *rushes into the room and picks it up for him.*

Hello, Carmody residence?

No, this is Tamsin. I should be on the –

Yeah.

He's here but you can talk to me.

She notices DEAN, *paralysed at the sink, glaring at her.*

(*Mouthing.*) Sorry.

DEAN. You didn't knock.

TAMSIN. Sorry, just a second –

　(*Whispering and covering the phone*.) We have to take this.

DEAN. Can't you take it in your room?

TAMSIN. I might need to ask you things.

　Okay?

　I wouldn't do it if I didn't need to.

DEAN (*gesturing to his hair*). I'm – doing this.

TAMSIN. Yeah, yeah, I know, but – I just think it sounds better if you're here. I won't make you talk to her, promise. You just – get on with your things. I won't look.

　(*Back into the phone*.) Okay, sorry, I'm back.

　Mm-hmm. Yeah yeah yeah.

　So –

　DEAN *tries to continue with his previous movements, but his hands are halting and he can't continue. It's gone wrong.*

　Wait, hang on, I thought you – have you already decided?

　DEAN *puts his head into the sink, and washes all the gel out of his hair.*

　I thought that was gonna be a different assessment though.

　Okay – okay, yeah, but –

　Okay. I didn't know you were allowed to do that.

　No, like, I get that and that's good of you to save him the time but no one told us that was the –

　But you're using one assessment to stop three totally different –

　Three, they said Carer's Allowance is linked to – yeah. Yeah yeah yeah.

　But they've still got different – requirements and –

Yeah I know, they said about the backlog but I just *said*, no one told us that –

Okay. I'm not – how soon are they gonna – stop?

Right. Okay. Um.

No that's just way – sooner than I –

DEAN *begins from scratch; same process as before.*

I'm aware of that.

Yes I'm aware we can do that but that's not what I'm –

No I'm calm, I'm totally calm, just that – look okay, I know this isn't anything to do with you but cos it's all of them at once, things aren't gonna add up unless –

Okay.

But that – he won't be able to do that though –

Look, why do you think it's me talking to you right now instead of him? He can't even use the phone, how do you expect him to do that consistently?

She mouths 'sorry' to DEAN *again. She tries to touch his shoulder and he dodges her.*

He tries to make for the door, but she swats him back to the sink and blocks his way.

He breathes angrily through his nose and grips the edge of the sink.

Are you sure? Cos I –

Okay. Right.

What's the like process for doing that? Is there like a form, or –

Oh. Okay. Okay.

I mean, we submitted everything the first time around. Like, the *same fucking stuff* that was okay before.

– I'm not swearing at *you*, I'm –

How long does that take, on average?

Can you give me a rough estimate. Please.

Okay. Okay. And can we get a copy of the report?

Can I come and collect it, or will you – ?

Okay.

Right. And can that be sent out today?

No, I'm just asking because –

Yeah. So it definitely will? Are you going to send it?

Sorry, no, obviously. Being stupid.

Okay. Yep.

Thanks for your – yeah. Okay.

She hangs up, and stares at the phone in her hand for a moment. She looks up at DEAN, *whose hand stutters when he senses her gaze.*

DEAN. Are you done?

TAMSIN. We should probably talk about…

　We need to figure out what to do.

DEAN. Can I just have a break for a bit?

TAMSIN. Dean…

DEAN. You've been in here for ages, I need to –

TAMSIN. Two minutes, and I haven't even been watching, / I've been

DEAN. I can *feel you looking*. I need you to just go away for a second so I can…

He gestures with the comb.

TAMSIN. What?

　DEAN *makes a keening noise of frustration.*

　…what?

DEAN. Finish this.

Come *on*.

TAMSIN *sighs*.

TAMSIN. How long do you want?

Half an hour?

DEAN.... an hour.

TAMSIN. Okay. I'll come in in an hour.

Pacified, DEAN *starts back at work on his hair.* TAMSIN *is just about to leave, when a sudden blast of music comes from next door.*

Fucking –

She bangs her fist on the wall. After a few moments the volume goes down to a hum, but it's too late.

DEAN *starts washing his hair out again.*

DEAN. Gimme an hour and a half. Six-thirty.

TAMSIN. Can we aim for an hour?

Cos we were gonna try and limit / how long we spent on this

DEAN. I *know*, but today has been –

TAMSIN. I know. I do get that.

Um. Did you get from the call that they've – ?

Beat.

Well, it's – it's a no on ESA. But it's also that they've used the assessment results / to

DEAN. You said I could have a break.

TAMSIN. I know.

DEAN. I don't wanna talk about this.

TAMSIN. I'm just – I just need to say it to process it.

We can still ask for the mandatory reconsideration.

Pause. No response from DEAN.

But it's just that we're not gonna get anything while they do that. They'll – what did they say – they'll *backdate it if they reinstate the claim.*

I should be a lawyer, I swear.

And cos that'll take a couple of weeks at least, they said you should apply for JSA.

DEAN. But I'm not meant to be / working.

TAMSIN. I know, I know, I don't even… they said you can get it on some temporary-hardship thing even if you're under eighteen.

DEAN. But what will they make me do?

TAMSIN. I mean. If we get the ESA back you won't have to do anything, but.

I think you probably just have to prove that you're – trying, and things.

DEAN. You mean go to sessions.

TAMSIN. – yeah.

Pause.

DEAN. Can you pass me my hat?

TAMSIN *takes a baseball cap from the hook on the door.*

DEAN *towel-dries his hair, and tries not to show his hair as he removes the towel and puts on the cap. He puts the towel over the mirror.*

TAMSIN. How… active do you feel?

DEAN. I don't wanna go anywhere.

TAMSIN. Because you just don't feel like it or because rules?

DEAN. Rules.

TAMSIN. All right, if you – if you try and relax tonight then I'll go with you to the Jobcentre tomorrow. Okay? And I'll – okay, I'll –

She takes a biro from her pocket and writes reminders on her hand.

…send the DWP a letter just reminding them that we've asked for a reconsideration…

She finishes writing and pauses for a second, trying to word this correctly.

The thing is. Um.

I don't know how long it's all gonna take, it might be weeks.

So I think I need to check in with my old agency and ask if they've got anything going.

Beat.

You can have a bit of alone-time.

DEAN. Why would you say that?

TAMSIN. I'm just –

Sorry. Stupid joke.

I might not get anything, just. If I do. I need to take it.

DEAN. Yeah.

TAMSIN. Are you okay?

DEAN. Yeah. Whatever.

He tries to turn away, finish the conversation.

Pause.

TAMSIN. Do you want a cup of tea?

Pause.

I'm being nice.

He eventually nods.

She goes into the kitchen, and puts the kettle on.

Once she's made the cup of tea, she brings it to DEAN *in the bathroom.*

He takes one sip and then immediately walks into the kitchen.

It's hot.

He doesn't listen, and puts it in the microwave for five seconds.

I promise you it's hot.

The microwave beeps, and DEAN *takes the tea out.*

TAMSIN *comes out of the bathroom and watches him – while trying to pretend that she isn't – as he takes another sip, and taps the counter twice with his left hand and twice with his right hand. He's trying to stave off an urge.*

It doesn't work, and he goes and microwaves the cup of tea again.

It's –

She stops herself.

She watches, for a few moments, before going into the bathroom.

She sits on the loo seat, takes a few moments to herself – and then takes a phone from her pocket, and makes a call.

Scene Two

TAMSIN *gets* DEAN *out of bed. It might take a while.*

TAMSIN. Come on.

*She gets each piece of his clothing as he checks his hair
between each one.*

Are we gonna have a good day?

DEAN *shrugs and shifts from foot to foot.*

Do you wanna – [tap]

Together TAMSIN *and* DEAN *tap each item of their
clothing four times, twice with the left hand and twice with
the right hand.*

Okay?

DEAN. Yeah.

TAMSIN. Are we gonna have a good day?

DEAN. Yes.

TAMSIN. Ten out of ten?

DEAN. I guess.

TAMSIN. Not 'I guess', that's a bit –

She thinks better of this.

Okay. Awesome. Your appointment's at four-thirty, / so if
you –

DEAN. I know.

TAMSIN. If you try and get as ready as you can this morning –
then I'll call you on my lunch and we can do some exercises
and get you out the door. Just if you can make sure you don't
put your headphones in –

DEAN. Why?

TAMSIN. Cos I dunno when I'll be able to call, okay?

Is that all right?

Pause.

DEAN. You can't ask me to do that. It's one of the only things /
that helps when I need to get ready to

TAMSIN. I know. I know. I know. But I don't wanna risk us
missing each other.

Can you do that for me, yeah?

Pause. DEAN *begins to tap again, but* TAMSIN *doesn't
join in.*

Dean. I have to go, I've gotta get all the way over to
Ridgmont. You need to pick up when I call, okay?

Speak to me. Okay?

DEAN. I hate that you're making me do this.

TAMSIN. I know. But promise me you're gonna answer.

Dean.

DEAN *exits; the* LEAD *enters.*

TAMSIN *hands him her passport.*

She completes a written test, and signs various forms.

She hands her papers and a urine sample to the LEAD, *who
also takes a swab from the inside of her cheek.*

The LEAD *gives her a high-vis vest and boots, which she
puts on.*

*In the moments before the lights come up on the fulfilment
centre,* TAMSIN *taps the vest and boots in the same way as
before – four times each, twice with the left and twice with
the right hand.*

LEAD. – and ideally, a target for this size will be four hundred
and eighty items per hour. That's eight items a minute, so
absolutely achievable, but we'll start you off on a target of
four hundred and see how you go. We have what we call the
'one best way' of packing – you saw that in the training video
– and each item you pack will be examined further down the
line, to check that it follows this method. Is that all clear?

TAMSIN. Yep.

LEAD. Have you done any packing work before?

TAMSIN *shakes her head.*

Which agency are you with?

TAMSIN. Quartz.

The name is familiar to him.

LEAD. Oh, Quartz. Okay –

He writes this down on a clipboard.

TAMSIN. Also I was wondering / how long

LEAD. What work have they given you before?

TAMSIN. Um, filing and data entry. / Two years ago.

LEAD. Okay. One moment, I just need to fill all this in.

So – there is a bit of terminology to take in but none of this
is difficult. If you work hard and you meet your targets,
there's always the possibility of transitioning to a permanent
associate post.

TAMSIN. Right.

LEAD. In your workstation – you've got the boxes here for
1A7, 1A5, A4, A1, B11 – there'll be other workers keeping
those boxes stocked for you – your scanner will tell you the
correct size for every item.

Right, we're a bit late starting, so if you don't have any
questions / I'll just

TAMSIN. I was just gonna ask about how long our break is, cos
I need to make a phone call and it / might take

LEAD. Have you got a phone on you?

TAMSIN. . . .yes?

LEAD. I'm gonna need to take it, I'm afraid.

You'll get it back at the end of the day, you just can't have it
on the floor.

TAMSIN *hands her phone over to him, slightly stunned.*

Anything else?

TAMSIN....no.

LEAD. All okay?

She takes too long to answer.

I've really got to go, but chin up, all right? See how you go.
I'll be back later.

TAMSIN *is left at her workstation, with* LUKE, *sixteen,
opposite her. They have a conveyer belt between them, on to
which they need to place the items they package.*

*Behind the workstation, a scoreboard of sorts can be seen.
On it we can see the time, a counter of the number of items*
TAMSIN *and* LUKE *have each packed so far in the hour,
and their current per-hour average.*

Currently the clock reads 07.16. TAMSIN*'s counters are
at 0.* LUKE*'s counter is at 96.*

TAMSIN *begins familiarising herself with the position of all
her equipment, and starts packing.*

After a long enough pause that it's a surprise:

LUKE. Have the boots got you yet?

TAMSIN. Sorry?

LUKE. The boots. They're crap.

TAMSIN. Oh.

LUKE. Or maybe the girls' boots are better, I dunno.

Long pause.

TAMSIN. How lo– sorry, can I ask you something?

LUKE. Yeah.

TAMSIN. How long is our lunch break?

LUKE. Half-hour.

TAMSIN. Okay. Um, and, also – where do they keep our phones and things?

LUKE. Keep packing.

TAMSIN. I just need / to know so I can

LUKE. No, it's fine, just they'll get the hump with you if you don't keep packing.

He probably gave it to security. They've got their office near the entrance.

TAMSIN. The entrance that way?

She points.

LUKE. Yep.

TAMSIN. The one fifteen minutes that way?

LUKE. Well. I did it once in thirteen but that was power-walking.

TAMSIN. And our break's half an hour.

LUKE. Co-rrect.

TAMSIN doesn't quite know how to respond to this. She continues packing.

After a moment:

TAMSIN. And if I needed to make a call?

LUKE. You can whistle for it.

TAMSIN. …right.

Pause. LUKE sees that his next item to package is an iPhone. He glances up at TAMSIN.

LUKE. Hey. Hey.

He has her attention – he lifts up the iPhone.

If only, eh?

TAMSIN. Don't, just.

Don't. Sorry.

LUKE. Okay, okay.

Just trying to lighten the mood.

The two of them package items in silence for thirty seconds or so, with TAMSIN's *counter on the wall automatically adjusting as she packs.*

She gets to grips with her masking-tape gun, and gets slightly quicker at the packaging as she goes.

The clock now reads 09.55. TAMSIN's *counter is at 243, with an average of 240 per hour.* LUKE's *counter is at 385, with an average of 420 per hour.*

TAMSIN *looks around all her cubbyholes for something that isn't there.*

TAMSIN. I don't have any 1A5s left.

I thought he said people would keep these stocked?

LUKE *checks his collection – none there either.*

LUKE. Oh, fucking hell.

TAMSIN *takes out a different size.*

No, don't, they'll notice. It'll rattle around, they'll just unpack it later.

She takes another item and tries to scan it. The scanner doesn't beep.

TAMSIN. It won't let me go to the next one.

What am I meant to do, just – wait?

LUKE. Er.

Looks like it.

TAMSIN. It'll look like I've just slacked off for five minutes.

LUKE. Once they bring them, you can catch up. Go faster.

TAMSIN. If I go any faster I'll make mistakes.

What happens if you don't make your targets?

LUKE. Depends.

TAMSIN. On what?

LUKE looks up at her and almost laughs.

LUKE. Don't look so serious!

Um, like, I think it depends on how many warnings you have?

Cos I mean, they don't just chuck you off as soon as you don't make target, but there are. Like. Things they do first. To try and make you meet targets. I dunno, I haven't had any of that happen yet.

He glances at his next item.

I swear this is like the fifth set of strawberry lube I've packaged in two days, I bet they're going to the same person.

He sees that TAMSIN is still worrying about her boxes not being available.

Try not to stress, yeah? They'll bring them.

TAMSIN. When?

LUKE. I don't know, do I? Jesus – look – you take over mine and I'll find where they've got to.

All right?

TAMSIN. Sure. Thanks.

LUKE only leaves his packing the moment TAMSIN takes over, making sure there's absolutely no gap in activity. At a light jog, he leaves the workstation.

While he's gone, TAMSIN tries to package his items as quickly as she can, while still looking worriedly at her empty spot opposite.

Her average begins dropping.

LUKE returns with an armful of 1A5 boxes.

LUKE. Bingo.

TAMSIN. Cheers.

He gives her half of the collection and she fits it into her cubbyhole.

TAMSIN *packages the item that had been waiting.*

When's our break?

LUKE. One.

TAMSIN. Sorry I know I just keep asking about lunch – I just, I do actually need to call someone, so.

LUKE. You're not gonna make it back before half-past.

TAMSIN. I'm gonna run, it'll be fine.

LUKE. Like – normally I'd say, all right, maybe chance it, but – you might get half a point for not packing anything while the 1A5s were out, right? So a whole point in one day – I wouldn't do it, man. It's better to like, really hold off on getting points till you get sick, cos that's when they, like, might just fire you if you've got too many points already.

Unless your phone call is, like, five seconds long. Then you might make it.

TAMSIN. They'd genuinely fire me?

LUKE. If it's in the next... how long do points last again?

Three months.

He shrugs.

I mean, it's your choice, but. I stopped trying to run places on my breaks cos it's just using up energy you're gonna need at like five o'clock when you're flagging.

He looks at his current item, a pair of slippers.

Hey, my mum has these.

The clock reads 12.59. TAMSIN's counter is at 245, with an average of 231 per hour. LUKE's counter is at 389, with an average of 404 per hour.

As the clock ticks over to 13.00 and a bell goes, TAMSIN *looks up, startled momentarily.* LUKE *steps away from his workstation.*

Stop stop stop.

TAMSIN *steps away from the item she was packing.*

Are you gonna try and make that call?

Pause.

TAMSIN *shakes her head.*

You okay?

TAMSIN *nods.*

Keep it together, yeah?

They don't want people who get all emotional. They think you'll bait them out or something.

TAMSIN. I'm fine.

LUKE. You / sure?

TAMSIN. Seriously, I'm fine.

TAMSIN *begins to walk away, then stops to ask:*

How far is the canteen?

LUKE. Ten minutes.

You can make it, just eat fast.

The clock reads 17.29. TAMSIN*'s counter is at 108, with an average of 228 per hour.* LUKE*'s counter is at 194, with an average of 400 per hour. As the clock turns over to 17.30, a closing bell tolls over the tannoy and they stop packing.*

Pause.

TAMSIN. Can we – ?

LUKE. Nah. Not till they say so.

Pause. LUKE *bounces on the balls of his feet impatiently.*

The line out's gonna be *so long* now. Fucking hell.

All the runners and problem-solvers just rush the doors and if you miss the moment right after the bell there's no point.

Fuck it.

He starts rummaging around inside his trousers.

TAMSIN.…what are you doing?

He emerges with some cigarettes.

Where'd you get those?

LUKE. I have connections in here, don't I?

…I just don't have a lighter. Bugger.

Here.

He offers one to her.

TAMSIN. Serious?

LUKE. Of course, I ain't gonna offer you one and then take it back, am I. Put it away before they see.

TAMSIN. Cheers.

She puts it in her pocket.

LUKE. I got mine in my pants.

TAMSIN.…

LUKE. So it's not there if my pockets get searched.

TAMSIN.…fair enough.

After a few moments that feel very long, the LEAD *enters.*

LEAD. This'll just take one moment.

He looks at his clipboard, and gets through his script as quickly as he can.

Luke. Luke Luke Luke. Right – you're not where we want you to be yet but you're up quite a bit, ninety per cent some of the time. Good stuff.

LUKE. Okay?

LEAD. You can come in tomorrow, right?

LUKE. Yep.

LEAD. Okay. On packing again, then. See you at seven.

LUKE. Sweet.

LUKE *leaves*.

LEAD. We've just got a bit of standard paperwork to get through at the end of each day. Performance-related, mainly.

TAMSIN. Okay.

LEAD. So, obviously this is your first day, but this is still a long way from your target.

TAMSIN. Yeah. I know. I spent five minutes waiting for 1A5 boxes to be replaced.

LEAD. It's quite a bit below what we'd expect from someone starting out, so, regardless of anything else affecting performance, we want the numbers to match up, okay?

TAMSIN....okay?

LEAD. I've also been told that you went to the toilet twice, and both times you didn't go to the one nearest your workstation.

TAMSIN. Which one is nearer?

LEAD. You went to the one on the west side. There's a closer one on the north-west side.

TAMSIN. I didn't know. They – the floor manager at the time didn't tell me where the nearest one was when I said I was going.

LEAD. I would be able to let you off if it was once, but since it's twice I have to give you a point.

TAMSIN. But you didn't tell me after the first time.

LEAD. I'm afraid it only got written up in the last hour. I hear you –

TAMSIN. It wasn't on purpose.

LEAD. I hear you –

TAMSIN. The only reason it's a point is to stop skiving and I wasn't, I went straight / back to my station

LEAD. I completely understand, but this is protocol. I can't justify not following it. To be honest, normally we'd be giving a point to someone when there's an obvious, extended period where they didn't pack a single item.

TAMSIN. Yeah, I said, / I was

LEAD. Normally we'd give a point for that. I can let you off because it's your first day. But I can't do that every time.

We do get a lot of people who aren't right for us. It's fine, because we have a large pool of agency workers to choose from, so if you want we can terminate this assignment now.

TAMSIN. I'm right for you.

LEAD. Okay.

I still have to give you a point.

TAMSIN. That's fine.

Can I come in tomorrow?

LEAD. How are your feet doing?

TAMSIN. Great.

Beat.

LEAD. We'll probably keep you on packing for now so you can come to this workstation again. Okay?

TAMSIN. Yep.

LEAD. You'll also want to put this –

He hands her phone back to her.

– in a locker on your way in tomorrow. You'll need to pay a deposit to be sure you'll have one available every day but it's worth it.

TAMSIN. Thanks.

*She puts it in her pocket and takes off her high-vis. Slowly –
she's too tired to keep rushing things.*

You have far to go to get home?

He keeps looking at his paperwork.

LEAD. That's it, you can go.

Beat.

She starts to leave.

Remember you can't take your jacket home with you. Leave
it hanging up.

She turns around, exiting in the opposite direction.

Scene Three

DEAN *and* TAMSIN*'s kitchen.*

DEAN *looks at the plate of food, with cling film over the top,
that* TAMSIN *has left for him. He peeps under the cling film for
a moment, and then tucks it back.*

He taps each item of his clothing and peels the cling film back.

He sets the plate a safe distance away from him, and taps again.

He picks up a fork, hesitantly, and spears a piece of food.

He puts the fork down.

He taps again.

He picks the fork up again.

He puts it down.

*He exits to go to the bathroom, where he spends about twenty
seconds on his hair ritual.*

He returns, and sits down.

He can't do it.

He tries to put the cling film back on the plate but the feel of the condensation on it makes him anxious. He puts it down and taps again.

He picks up the plate and puts it in the bottom drawer of a kitchen unit.

He returns to the bathroom, and starts doing his hair.

TAMSIN *enters, and takes her shoes off immediately. She sits down and kneads her feet through her socks.*

When she notices some letters, she pounces on them and opens them all up. None of them are the reconsideration result.

After a long pause, she hears the water running intermittently. Realises DEAN *is still up. She manages to force herself over to knock on the door.*

TAMSIN. Hey.

    Pause.

    'm sorry I didn't call. They took my phone away.

    Are you okay?

DEAN. I couldn't go outside.

TAMSIN. I know. I'm really sorry.

    Come out here and talk.

DEAN. No.

TAMSIN. I'm not angry with you.

DEAN. Why would you be angry with me? You wouldn't have any right to be angry with me.

TAMSIN. Okay. I just wanna know you're all right.

    Pause.

    TAMSIN *gets her phone out of her pocket and composes a text to* DEAN.

His phone vibrates – he picks it up and reads it.

He opens the door, coming out into the kitchen.

DEAN. I don't wanna read your stupid text, didn't you see how many times I called you?

She reaches out to his scalp. He avoids her touch.

Don't.

TAMSIN. You're bleeding –

DEAN. *Don't.*

TAMSIN. I didn't mean for you to –

DEAN. You rushed me this morning.

TAMSIN. Because I had to *go*. If you wanna wake up even earlier to give us more time, be my guest.

DEAN. I really wanted to be able to go out.

TAMSIN. I know. I wanted you to as well.

The Jobcentre didn't try and ring or anything?

DEAN *shakes his head.*

We should probably call them and – try and explain what happened. Might come to nothing, but.

DEAN. They're not open now.

TAMSIN. Shit. Yeah.

Beat, and then, slowly:

Would you be able to call / them tomorrow?

DEAN. No.

No.

TAMSIN. Dean, I'm not gonna be able to do it. I'm in work before they open, I get back after they close, I can't ring anyone all day –

DEAN. Neither can I.

TAMSIN. You've phoned people before. I've seen you do it. Don't tell me you *can't*.

DEAN. People I *know*. I won't be able to do anything else for the rest of the day –

TAMSIN. Yeah? What else is new?

Beat.

Sorry. Sorry.

Look, it's just. If we don't tell them straight away what happened then that's zero JSA for at least this week, probably longer cos I think we'd have to apply for the hardship bollocks all over again – and I don't even get paid till I've done two weeks. And I don't know if we still qualify for all the other things like council-tax reduction cos no one I asked would fucking say. Like it depends on my income and I don't even know what that's gonna be, and I just, I have this feeling they might just hit us with a massive fucking bill maybe even going back all the way to your assessment date or something.

DEAN. How likely is that?

TAMSIN. I dunno, do I? That's what I'm saying.

We can try and – leave them a message or something. Maybe see if they can arrange to call you or something, but you'd have to promise to answer…

She looks around.

Where's the folder?

Did you move it?

DEAN *says nothing*.

She starts looking in drawers.

Can't ever find anything in this place, you put something down and it just *vanishes*…

DEAN. Don't –

Too late. She opens the drawer with the plate in.

TAMSIN. Oh Jesus.

  You didn't eat *any* of it?

DEAN. I'm going to.

TAMSIN. You're not 'going to', it's in the fucking *drawer.*

DEAN. I was gonna leave it there until I felt ready to / eat it

TAMSIN. It'll be cold.

DEAN. I can microwave it, can't I?

TAMSIN. No, you can't reheat rice, it goes all / funny

DEAN. Then I don't understand why you made me rice!

TAMSIN. Because it's cheap. That's why.

  And I thought it'd be – safe. Y'know. It's bland.

  I dunno, you can spend bloody hours on your hair –

DEAN. Shut up, shut *up* –

TAMSIN. On your hair, let's be clear about that, on your *hair* –
  and you weren't even outside all day – couldn't you at least
  have *tried*?

DEAN. I did.

TAMSIN. Okay. Whatever.

DEAN. I *did*.

  TAMSIN *shrugs, opening the bin to get rid of the food.*

  You don't have to do that.

TAMSIN. Are you gonna eat it?

  Pause. DEAN *doesn't answer.*

  Then yeah, I do have to do this.

  She makes to start throwing it away and then can't do it.

  No. No.

  She starts to eat some of it herself.

  I'm not fucking wasting anything else.

There's nothing wrong with it. You know that.

DEAN *starts pulling at a few strands of his hair.*

Stop *doing* that, you're gonna –

She tries to pull DEAN's *hand away from his hair, and he moves out of the way.*

Look, this –

She goes into the bathroom and gets a pot of DEAN's *gel.*

– this –

DEAN. DON'T.

TAMSIN (*opening it up and scooping gel on to her hand*). It's shit. I fucking hate looking at it.

DEAN. Give it back.

TAMSIN. What does it even do??

This is why I'm too bloody scared to check your bank account, cos I don't even know how much of this you've bought and hidden away.

DEAN. I'm saving it.

TAMSIN. For *what*??

DEAN. Just give it *back*.

Beat – and then TAMSIN *does.*

DEAN *clutches the pot in his hand really hard, has to stop himself from throwing it.*

He goes into the bathroom and locks the door.

TAMSIN. Oh yeah, that's great. Do that.

He begins to apply more gel to his hair.

Beat. She calls through the door:

I'm sorry.

Look – I'm just saying – we can't afford to waste food.

Still through the door:

DEAN. You don't have to spend money getting me food.

TAMSIN. Yes I do, this is the only thing I'm putting my foot down on, / the only thing –

DEAN. You don't –

TAMSIN. – you can do whatever you like with the – the hair and things, but you have to eat.

DEAN. It's not that I don't want to, just –

TAMSIN. What?

No answer.

What is it?

DEAN. Look, I'm not gonna talk about it to you, okay? It's private, and –

TAMSIN. But food's not – it's not a flexible thing, I can't write it off again and go, oh, okay, we'll talk about that in a few months' time, cos look where that got us, / it's your actual *life* here –

DEAN *has been getting more and more frustrated with his hair.*

DEAN. Can you just shut up? I need to concentrate here and you're just – making everything worse – I need you to fuck off for like ten fucking minutes for once – is that like too much for you or something –

TAMSIN. You have *no idea* how much I just wanna leave you to it sometimes. No fucking idea. You should be thanking your lucky fucking *stars* that I haven't because I really, really want to sometimes.

…

Sorry. Sorry. I'm just tired, I've – I've had a shit day, we've both had shit days.

Dean.

She gives up, and is still and exhausted for a few moments.

Then she slowly gets up to wash the gel off her hands, and wash the plate.

After she's finished, she wipes her hands on her jeans, and feels something in her pocket. She reaches inside and takes out the cigarette.

An idea.

She knocks on the bathroom door gently.

No answer.

I've got something for you, I forgot.

DEAN. What?

TAMSIN. Open the door.

Beat.

DEAN *opens the door a crack.*

She shows him the cigarette.

DEAN. Who gave you that?

TAMSIN. Guy at work.

DEAN. Why?

TAMSIN. I dunno – look, do you wanna smoke it or not?

DEAN. It's yours.

TAMSIN. Can share.

She takes a box of matches out of a drawer, then lights the cigarette.

She takes one puff, just managing to stop herself from coughing, and taking care to waft the smoke away, before offering it to DEAN.

It's fine, honestly.

DEAN *comes out of the bathroom, and takes the cigarette from* TAMSIN. *He taps it twice with his left hand and twice with his right hand. Then he takes a drag.*

Good?

DEAN *nods.*

They're meant to calm you down, aren't they? I don't know if it's chemical or just your imagination but I think they're meant to.

I've just had a really bad day.

Beat.

DEAN (*as though it's a stock phrase*). 'You and me both, kiddo.'

TAMSIN. Yeah.

Beat.

I'm gonna ask about food again.

DEAN. I can't – if we need to talk about it I need to –

TAMSIN. What?

You wanna do what Mum used to do?

He nods.

I thought you'd moved past – no, fine. Do me a list of things you'll be okay with.

He does, and gives it to her.

She underlines one or more of them.

So if I got you these that'd be okay?

DEAN. If they're –

TAMSIN. I'll do them totally plain, yeah. And you'd have it again tomorrow?

DEAN....

TAMSIN. I need to keep thirty quid for the bus in case I get five days this week. We can't squeeze for anything extra tomorrow.

Beat.

These are good, they're completely good for you. Fibre and protein and things.

Long pause.

What are you worried about?

DEAN. You know how you were at work today.

TAMSIN. Yeah?

DEAN. How much are they paying you?

TAMSIN. Five-fifty an hour.

Beat.

DEAN. If you earn too much doesn't that stop us from getting the hardship JSA?

TAMSIN *pauses and freezes for a moment. Thinking it through.*

TAMSIN. I don't know.

It's in your name and not mine, and I've not got contracted hours anyway, so… maybe not? But it might be based on the hours you actually end up working so…

Pause.

Okay, um – when I read some of the stuff about the hardship JSA I couldn't work out if we actually qualified anyway, cos it said you had to not be living with a parent or someone acting as your parent. But they know the situation. We've not hidden anything.

Look – you don't have to worry about it, yeah? I'll handle it. Just focus on doing all the stuff on the agreement thing you signed. Okay?

DEAN *shrugs.*

Did you move the folder?

DEAN *starts tapping, almost indiscernibly.*

Did you lose it?

It's okay if you did, we can – maybe we can ask them to post us another diary and things?

Before he can speak, DEAN *goes to rearrange his hair very quickly.*

TAMSIN *waits.*

DEAN *returns, and goes to a cupboard and takes out a cardboard folder, which is under some plates.*

He taps it eight times with his left hand and eight times with his right hand, and goes to put it on the table next to TAMSIN.

DEAN *returns to the bathroom and checks his hair again.*

He returns to the table and sits down.

In an attempt at levity:

I really thought you had lost it. You totally had me going.

She opens it and flips through the Jobseeker's Diary inside.

Okay.

This is all really different to the ESA stuff. Um.

So these are the commitments you agreed with them?

DEAN. Yeah.

TAMSIN. Have you done any of them?

Pause.

Did you try?

DEAN. Yeah.

TAMSIN. What happened?

DEAN. I can't look at this stuff for too long without...

Beat.

TAMSIN. I know.

DEAN. They said I had to make a CV and, like, I did try and start, but.

TAMSIN. What?

DEAN. What would you put in one? If you were me?

TAMSIN. Your – skills, and things. Your grades.

DEAN *isn't impressed with this answer.*

You've got your C in Maths.

You know that if you went to Bletchley they'd help you with this stuff.

Beat.

DEAN. Did you have to mention that?

TAMSIN. Okay, okay. I'm sorry.

DEAN. For fuck's sake.

I don't even wanna be doing this in the first place. I'm putting all this effort in and you just like mess with me like that.

TAMSIN. Sorry. Look –

DEAN. I'm in this – bad cycle / anyway –

TAMSIN. Five more minutes. Come on. Please. Let's get this done and then you can do whatever you need.

DEAN. No, I can't, cos I'll have to – eat.

Beat.

TAMSIN. I get how hard this is. I do. I know I'm asking a lot.

D'you remember when I Blu-Tacked your revision stuff all over the walls? Would that help?

DEAN. With what?

TAMSIN. The commitments.

DEAN. No.

TAMSIN. No?

DEAN. I don't wanna see it everywhere, that'll... yeah.

TAMSIN. All right, I'm gonna – I'm gonna write down all your commitments here so it's not on the diary, we don't have to get the folder out at all – and you can organise this how you like, doesn't have to be my way – and we'll just, we'll set a time when we try and do a few of them every night.

DEAN. I'll be worried about it all day, though.

TAMSIN. We won't get it done otherwise. You know we won't.

That sound okay?

DEAN *shrugs*.

Yeah?

DEAN. Yeah. Fine.

TAMSIN. I'll send a letter to the Jobcentre and say we're doing that. Maybe – take photos or something. As evidence.

DEAN. I tried to look at applications. Online ones.

TAMSIN. Yeah?

DEAN. But they always ask about gaps, where you weren't working or in school.

TAMSIN. ...yeah. Right.

I guess you say you were too ill.

DEAN. Are you sure?

Beat.

TAMSIN. I mean, you can't lie, can you? There are – records that you've been on ESA. I mean you can say that the council exempted you from college and things.

If you don't say anything they'll think you've been in prison.

DEAN. They're not gonna hire me either way.

TAMSIN. But it's not – you just have to prove that you're applying, don't you? For now? In the 'outcome' section you can put, I dunno, 'I have tried applying for things but don't know what to say about gaps.'

DEAN....

TAMSIN. I know that sounds crap.

Maybe you should put some jokes in there. Liven it up.

Pause.

How're we gonna organise this, then? Do you wanna keep it with the ESA and PIP stuff or is that gonna be confusing?

DEAN. If we put it all in order it'll be fine.

TAMSIN. Cool, I'll go get the box –

She exits, calling behind her:

Is it still in my room?

DEAN. Yeah.

TAMSIN *re-enters, carrying a box full of papers, neatly divided.*

TAMSIN. Here we go. Okay, that's last year... this year is... all here... so we can put it with that.

DEAN. Oh – wait –

He separates some sheets from the Jobcentre packet.

These are ESA things.

TAMSIN. Are they?

DEAN. It's the report.

TAMSIN. Seriously? What does it say?

She takes the sheets and starts reading.

DEAN. I haven't looked, when it arrived I – didn't want / to –

TAMSIN. Blah blah blah – 'Can get dressed without help or aids'.

...did you say that?

DEAN. No, they asked – they asked if there was any – like, physical disability that stopped me getting dressed. And I said no, but that I needed you to help me.

TAMSIN. 'Is able to go to local shops most days'… 'experiences no distress when interacting with unfamiliar people'. This is bollocks, this is all bollocks, these are just *lies*.

Did they say this was what they were writing? Did they not let you explain?

DEAN. I didn't wanna fiddle with my hair in the assessment so I sat on my hands – and then I couldn't – (*Gestures to mean 'tap'*.) so it was really hard to, like, concentrate on what I was saying.

Beat.

TAMSIN. Was it a man?

DEAN. What?

TAMSIN. Was it a man who did your assessment, or was it a woman?

Beat.

DEAN. It was a man.

TAMSIN. Good-looking?

DEAN. Yeah.

TAMSIN. Good hair?

DEAN *shrugs. Sort of nods.*

Beat.

I should have gone in with you.

DEAN. It's not your fault.

TAMSIN. Yeah, but.

I should've managed all this better. Cos I knew they'd be harsh. I just. I didn't think they'd lie.

Okay, um, I'm gonna – I'm gonna look at every bit that's not true and write what it's actually like and how the rituals mean you can't do any of this. And send that as a new piece of evidence for the reconsideration. And if they say you have to have another assessment I'll go in with you.

DEAN. I don't like you saying 'rituals'.

TAMSIN. I know. Sorry. They won't understand otherwise, y'know?

DEAN gets up.

DEAN. Um, can I – ?

TAMSIN. Sorry, I know this is a bit – intense.

DEAN. I just need to –

TAMSIN. It's fine, go ahead.

He goes to the bathroom and closes the door. Takes some deep breaths and spends a while cutting bits of his hair.

He opens the door but still stands in the bathroom, talking to TAMSIN *from there.*

DEAN. Is this gonna work?

Beat.

TAMSIN. They cut you off thinking you had nothing wrong with you, that's the thing. Like, *I* would look at this report and go 'Okay, clearly they're fine.' I reckon we send this off, they get you in for another assessment – and I'll – get some hours off work and go with you – and we're golden.

DEAN. Really?

TAMSIN. Yeah. We know what we're getting into this time, we know what they're looking for.

I'll finish this off and then are you okay to eat?

DEAN. Mm.

He doesn't approach TAMSIN, *but holds his hand out.*

High-five.

TAMSIN *grins and gets up, goes over to him and gently returns his high-five.* DEAN *exits.*

She returns to annotate the pages of the report, but before she can really start she's back at her workstation in the warehouse. LUKE *is already there. The clock reads 06.58.*

LUKE (*jokily*). We gotta stop meeting like this!

TAMSIN (*looking up*). Hm?

LUKE. Just – saying hi.

TAMSIN. Hi. Sorry, it's – I'm really tired.

Beat.

I had a late one last night. Not a – fun late one, just.

Yeah.

LUKE. Didja notice that this road – the, um, the one we're on – is called Badgers Rise?

Jokes, right? I lived in MK all my life and I ain't never seen no badger about.

Beat.

What's your name again?

TAMSIN. Tamsin.

LUKE. Luke.

I'd shake your hand but – cardboard cuts.

TAMSIN. Oh – yeah. Me too.

Pause.

The time crawls closer and closer to seven. As it approaches:

Should we –

The LEAD *enters.*

LEAD. Morning.

How are we feeling?

If we can get started –

Tamsin – two hundred and twenty-eight an hour average yesterday – now you're used to everything we need to try and make four hundred.

TAMSIN. Right.

LEAD. Do you think you can do it?

TAMSIN. – yeah. Sure.

LEAD. Four hundred then.

(*To* LUKE.) So you've just about managed your initial target, but most people by this time have managed to bump that up to the mid-four-hundreds at least. So I need you to try and push your rate up to four hundred and fifty, or at least consistently four hundred and twenty or above, okay?

LUKE. Okay.

LEAD. Orders are tailing off a little bit at this point in the month so it should be easy.

TAMSIN. When –

The LEAD *looks at her, slightly startled by the interruption.*

– sorry – um – when do we know, like on average, if we'll be working tomorrow? Do you like – decide based on orders or performance / or

LEAD. I'm gonna get back to you on that, okay? Right now I don't know.

TAMSIN. Okay. Cos I'm definitely available.

LEAD. Sure.

TAMSIN. Just so you know.

Beat.

LEAD. We'll have a little chat in a few hours.

He exits. TAMSIN *and* LUKE *start packing – trying to make up for the minute they've just lost.* TAMSIN *redoes her hair tie and winces.*

LUKE. They've only ever told me at the end of the day. Or sometimes the agency texts the next morning.

TAMSIN. Do you get used to them?

LUKE. What, the leads?

TAMSIN. Well, them too, but I meant – the, uh, cardboard cuts.

LUKE. Oh. Nah, they just get opened up again. I bet I'm gonna have scars, I'm gonna make out I been in a fight...

Pause.

TAMSIN. Can we ask them to open the doors?

LUKE. ?

TAMSIN. Aren't you hot?

LUKE thinks for a second.

LUKE. I've never seen them open the doors on-shift.

Probably worried about theft and that. Fucking everything's about theft.

He sees his next order: it's a vibrator.

Ohhh this is what I like to see first thing in the morning, man.

He shows her.

TAMSIN. I'm like half-asleep, I can't deal with that right now.

He waves it closer to her like it's something gross. She can't help but crack a tiny smile, just cos of how stupid it is.

Get it away!

He's already got it away – he can't afford to package it too slowly.

LUKE. It's called a Humdinger, what does that do?

TAMSIN. I dunno, do I?

LUKE. What, you mean you don't have like, five of them at home?

TAMSIN. Sorry. I'm not that up on sex-toy trends.

LUKE. Oh, well, you work here a few weeks and you'll see loads.

I'm just like preparing you in advance cos they get really weird.

Do people call you Taz?

TAMSIN. No.

LUKE. I bet they do.

She gives him a look.

(*Still bright and unfazed.*) I'm gonna shut up.

TAMSIN. I dreamt about this last night. I dreamt that I was packing boxes in boxes in boxes.

LUKE. I had that after my first day, but it was the – beeping.

Cos I was on picking. They have a different beep on their scanners and after ten hours it gets in your head.

TAMSIN. How's picking?

LUKE. Man. I was like in a trance or something I swear. I don't even remember half of it, you could tell me I passed out and I'd believe you.

TAMSIN. Shit.

LUKE. Yeah.

TAMSIN. Is this better?

LUKE. Nah. Just bad in a different way.

The clock reads 09.31. TAMSIN's counter is at 128, with an average of 249 per hour. LUKE's counter is at 212, with an average of 430.

TAMSIN finishes packing an item, and it's clear she feels slightly faint. She takes a moment to breathe deeply before she takes her next item.

The LEAD enters. He might swear to himself in his own language as he approaches – he's just had a bollocking.

LEAD. Right, guys. We're only two and a half hours in and I've been told there's a pretty big shortfall over here. Tamsin – you have to step up, okay?

TAMSIN. Okay.

LEAD (*indicating* LUKE). He's almost doubling you right now.

TAMSIN. Yeah.

LEAD. So it's not impossible, is it?

TAMSIN. No.

LEAD. It's not impossible.

TAMSIN....no, it's not impossible.

LEAD. Keep positive about it, okay? You've got a good work ethic and that's great, but whatever you think is the limit you can do, raise it.

TAMSIN. Okay. Yep. Sure.

LEAD. I'll be back soon.

The LEAD *exits*.

LUKE. You okay?

TAMSIN. It's too hot.

LUKE. Keep going, just be a robot for a bit.

TAMSIN. I think I'm gonna – / I can't –

LUKE. Are you gonna faint?

TAMSIN. – what do I do?

LUKE *looks around, checks no supervisors are nearby*.

LUKE. Um, there's a water fountain, right – if you run it's like two minutes that way.

TAMSIN. But I won't –

LUKE. Leg it. I'll cover you.

TAMSIN. Thanks. Thanks.

As in Scene Two, LUKE *takes over* TAMSIN*'s work so there is no gap in activity.* TAMSIN *runs off.*

The clock reads 12.58. TAMSIN*'s counter is at 245, with an average of 251 per hour.* LUKE*'s counter is at 429, with an average of 436.*

TAMSIN *is back.* LUKE *struggles with a very large and heavy bag.*

He checks the label.

LUKE. It's couscous.

This is forty kilogram of couscous, why would you need that much couscous?

TAMSIN. Wow.

I mean I had twelve MAC lipsticks all going to one person yesterday, so. People bulk buy all sorts.

LUKE. *Couscous* though?!

TAMSIN. Maybe that's the only food they can manage.

LUKE. But forty kilogram at once, the label says it's fifty quid! Though I guess it's cheaper from here.

TAMSIN. But I mean, maybe they can't eat anything else.

LUKE. Oh. Right. Like allergies?

Man, now I'm depressed.

TAMSIN. Try saying 'couscous' again.

The clock ticks over to 13.00 and the bell goes. TAMSIN *checks her numbers.*

Fuck.

How are you doing four hundred?

LUKE. You'll get faster.

TAMSIN. Like, today?

LUKE. If there's the work they'll ask you back tomorrow. Don't stress your numbers, like.

TAMSIN. Are you going to the canteen?

LUKE. Nah, I want a full half-hour sitting down.

TAMSIN. You're not gonna eat?

LUKE. Had a massive fry-up and a Red Bull before coming –
doing an experiment, gonna see if that gets me through.

*He sits on his workstation, and takes his boots off, throwing
them on the floor, before lying down.*

Oh man that's so good. I am really sorry if they smell but
that feels so good.

Tell me if you see anyone coming, yeah?

TAMSIN *leans against her workstation, and examines her
fingers for cardboard cuts.*

The clock reads 13.15.

LUKE *gets off the workstation, and puts his boots back on.*

Right, your turn.

TAMSIN. Hmm?

LUKE. Sit down. I'll keep watch.

TAMSIN. …you sure?

LUKE. Yeah, course – go go go, it's already sixteen past!
Thirteen minutes!

TAMSIN *sits on her workstation.*

Take your boots off – seriously, it's amaze.

TAMSIN *unlaces her boots and takes them off. It's obviously
a relief.*

Pause.

What were you doing before this?

TAMSIN. Oh, we're doing twenty questions.

LUKE. Nah. It's just, you get all sorts here, so I ask.

TAMSIN. Yeah.

She looks around her for something to help change the subject.

Hey, look.

She holds up a Bat Out of Hell II *vinyl that was on the bottom of her next order.*

LUKE. What's that?

TAMSIN. Oh come on.

LUKE. It looks like some goth shit?

TAMSIN. It's Meat Loaf!

LUKE. *What?*

TAMSIN. You know. 'Bat Out of Hell'. 'I'd Do Anything for Love'.

(*Singing.*) 'I would do anything for love – '

Seeing LUKE*'s expression:*

No? Okay.

LUKE. 'Meat Loaf'?!

TAMSIN. Yeah.

LUKE. That his actual name?

TAMSIN. …I dunno. I guess not. But he's – oh my god he's so great. He's like completely, gloriously over the top. Classic power rock.

LUKE. Not my kinda thing.

TAMSIN. Yeah, see, I thought that, but he gets you. Just wait, sit through a few tracks and he gets you.

LUKE. Lemme see?

She hands him the vinyl.

TAMSIN. It's like… pure joy. I promise.

LUKE. I'll check him out later.

TAMSIN. Yeah?

She laughs, and lies down on the workstation.

Report back, tell me what you think.

Pause.

You're so right about badgers, y'know?

LUKE. Right?!

TAMSIN. Never seen one in my life.

Badgers Rise.

LUKE. Yeah, like, rising from *where*??

TAMSIN *laughs, and holds up the vinyl again.*

TAMSIN. Out of hell. Obviously.

The clock reads 17.30. TAMSIN's counter is at 126, with an average of 247 per hour. LUKE's counter is at 204, with an average of 410 per hour.

The LEAD is already present. He looks tired.

I know. I know.

I just need to get used to it all. I can do better.

LEAD. Carmody.

TAMSIN holds her hand up. He gives her a sheet of paper.

Mburu.

LUKE *receives one too.*

These are your scores from today. It's a breakdown, so you can see – right there is your average for each hour, and your average overall, and then the target, and what percentage you've fallen behind.

Take it home and think through how you can improve, all right?

TAMSIN. Sure.

LEAD. So there's not really any excuse for you not to be reaching your targets. Okay?

She nods. He turns to LUKE.

So, a few hours where you hit a hundred-per-cent target, but then that tailed off a lot towards the end of the day, so you need to work on that.

And there's a period – here – where your usual standard, and the standard we want, really slipped – a, a five-minute interval where we didn't record any activity.

LUKE. Right.

LEAD. What was going on there?

LUKE. Back ache. Had to have a stretch.

LEAD. Sure. It's not really acceptable after being here a few months, so I'm gonna need to give you half a point for it.

LUKE. Won't happen again.

That answer's a relief.

LEAD. Brilliant. Brilliant. Okay.

Right.

Can both of you keep tomorrow free?

LUKE. Yeah.

TAMSIN. – Yeah. Yeah.

LEAD. All right. Come in for seven and we'll see how many people we end up needing.

The LEAD *exits.* TAMSIN *and* LUKE *begin unlacing their boots.*

TAMSIN. Sorry, I shouldn't have / let you

LUKE. Bruv. Not like I care. I'm leaving soon.

Is Carmody your last name?

TAMSIN. Oh. Yeah.

LUKE. D'you know Dean Carmody?

Beat.

TAMSIN. Why?

LUKE. Year above me at school. Is he your cousin or?

TAMSIN. – he's my younger brother.

LUKE. Ohhh yeah, you're *old*, I forgot.

TAMSIN. Yeah, yeah, shut up.

LUKE. He's seriously your brother?

TAMSIN. I know he's…

LUKE. What?

She shrugs.

TAMSIN. I dunno.

LUKE. How come I never saw you at school?

TAMSIN. I went to Collier.

LUKE. Oh right.

Hartley wasn't bad, y'know.

TAMSIN. Yeah, but he didn't really…

She thinks better of it.

You know what, I should probably get going, / I need to

LUKE. No, I get what you mean. He was kinda –

TAMSIN (*cutting him off before he can find the words*). I need to get back.

LUKE. But, like, I was in detention with him once and you could tell he was smart.

Like I think it was History work or something, someone was doing their head in over a source question and he just got it, like instantly, and he kind of talked them through it till they understood.

Pause. This is something TAMSIN *can't imagine now.*

TAMSIN. Cool.

Pause.

Want me to take your things out too?

Save you a trip.

LUKE *hands her his jacket and boots.*

LUKE. Cheers, bruv.

TAMSIN. See you soon.

She leaves. LUKE *starts walking the opposite way.*

LUKE. Same time? Same place?

TAMSIN. Don't even joke.

Scene Four

A week later. TAMSIN *is packing at her workstation, alone. The clock reads 16.27.* TAMSIN's *counter is at 121, with an average of 243 items per hour.*

TAMSIN *is going faster than we've seen her so far. She packs for just long enough that the lack of dialogue starts to feel strange.*

And then one of her packages contains a yoga DVD. She takes a moment, while getting the box, to look at the back of the DVD.

TAMSIN. Downward Dog.

She packs it.

LUKE *swings by, possibly riding on his trolley. (But not for too long. He's breaking lots of health and safety rules.)*

LUKE. All right Tammifer?

Tammalamadingdong?

How's it going?

TAMSIN. Where've you been?

LUKE. Ahhh you missed me!

TAMSIN. I've been by myself for days, I've missed humans.

LUKE. Yeah yeah.

TAMSIN. Seriously, I packed a football and had to stop myself stealing it and drawing a face on it.

Where've you been?

LUKE. Picking, right? They were short – needed a big strong boy like me to fill in.

TAMSIN. They said that, did they?

LUKE. Nah, course not.

Pause.

You know how I said packing and picking were equal levels of shit?

Picking is worse. I've decided.

TAMSIN. Right.

LUKE. It's the muscles.

I wish I could have headphones.

TAMSIN. Oh god, me too. That'd be so good.

LUKE. How's it been over here?

TAMSIN. Shit. Fucking shit. Broke three hundred a few times yesterday but I'm not even making two hundred and fifty now.

LUKE. Just remember that the only limitations are the limitations you set for yourself.

TAMSIN *makes a face.*

Arrggh, it burns!

TAMSIN. Yeah, that's right, you don't wanna see my angry face.

There's some writer who said women on their periods could kill bees just by looking at them. My teacher told me.

LUKE. Ah, that stuff's all wank. My mum, like, when she's on her period she just gets sad, not angry. Extra cup of tea and she's fine.

Why, are you…?

TAMSIN. What? No. No.

She looks at the scoreboard. Her average has gone down to 230.

Look, they're so gonna tick you off for standing around.

LUKE *takes a quick look around, making for his scanner again so he can look busy – but his hand cramps and stutters when he tries to pick it up.*

You okay?

LUKE. Yeah, I'm –

His hand gets stuck in a loop of cramping.

I'm fine –

TAMSIN. Hold it up.

He holds up his hand. TAMSIN presses her palm flat against LUKE's – he winces as his fingers bend back.

I know. I know.

Push against it.

He does – and she pushes back, letting him stretch his fingers against it.

Did that work?

LUKE. – yeah. Cheers.

Least I'm gonna be hench by the end of the day, right?

TAMSIN. Oh, totally.

LUKE. One of the other guys said he lost a stone in his first month of picking. And he's *old*, like.

TAMSIN. Sorry, I don't wanna be – I really need to keep going, they're kinda losing patience with me.

Beat.

I don't want them to get pissed off with you.

LUKE. I do.

Well, not really. But. Sometimes. Days like this.

TAMSIN. Yeah. I know what you mean.

LUKE. Yeah.

Beat.

He braves a look at his scanner, and winces.

I'm so gonna get a point for this. I shoulda been at north side one minute twenty seconds ago. Twenty-five seconds. Twenty-six.

Pause. In for a penny, in for a pound.

Let's go to the pub.

TAMSIN. What?

LUKE. Not *now*. Obviously. Tomorrow. Or when we both have a day off.

TAMSIN. – I –

LUKE. All my mates have gone Amsterdam. Did some bus deal online and got ten-pound tickets. And I'm here, doing this. I wanna go pub tomorrow.

TAMSIN. Look I can't – I can't think about this right now, I've gotta –

I have to keep going.

LUKE. Okay. Sound.

He begins to wheel his cart away, but has a sudden thought and rummages in his pocket.

Here.

He presents TAMSIN *with a single tealight – he might even chuck it at her so she has to catch it.*

Enjoy. Bag of a thousand tealights split open so I'm guessing they can't sell 'em.

He continues wheeling his cart away.

TAMSIN (*hissing*). Where am I gonna put this?

LUKE *looks around, mouths 'in your shirt' and makes hand gestures.* TAMSIN *puts it inside her shirt, fitting it into her bra and trying not to laugh.* LUKE *starts to wheel his cart away again.*

(*Only half-joking.*) Don't leave me here!

Scene Five

TAMSIN *is waiting outside a pub near her house. It's really warm, a kind of golden late-summer evening.* TAMSIN *could look a bit different here – clothes we haven't seen before, maybe, or wearing her hair down.*

LUKE *approaches.* TAMSIN *shields her eyes from the sun.*

LUKE. Heyy.

TAMSIN. Hey! Hi. Sorry, I can't –

She shifts herself slightly so the sun isn't in her eyes as much.

Hi.

You okay?

LUKE. Yeah, yeah.

TAMSIN. Um I thought we could – sit here / cos it's –

LUKE. Yeah, yeah –

TAMSIN. So warm and that.

LUKE. Yeah.

He tries to find a position where the sun isn't in his eyes too much, and sits.

Pause.

TAMSIN. Was it okay –

She gestures.

LUKE. Getting here?

TAMSIN. Yeah. Sorry for making you come to my neck of the woods.

LUKE. Oh, nah – why would you wanna come to Conniburrow, like?! – I'm just late cos I got kinda tied up at home.

TAMSIN. Sure, sure.

Pause.

Everything all right?

LUKE. All – ?

TAMSIN. At home.

LUKE. Oh – yeah. Yeah. Just stuff.

Pause.

TAMSIN. It's weird, I kinda didn't recognise you.

LUKE. Yeah?

TAMSIN. You know, without the – without the vest.

LUKE. Ohh.

I think I really work the high-vis, y'know?

TAMSIN. Oh definitely, yeah.

Totally brings out your eyes.

LUKE. Yeah, my bright orange eyes.

Pause.

TAMSIN. Um. I was gonna say – d'you wanna…

Beat.

LUKE. What?

TAMSIN. D'you wanna buy me a drink?

LUKE. Oh. Uh –

TAMSIN. You don't have to.

LUKE. No, like, it's fine, but I'm six/teen

TAMSIN. Sixteen.

Fuck, yeah, I forgot.

Pause.

Would they actually ID you though?

LUKE. I dunno, I ain't been here before – look, I'll give you the change and you go get us both something.

He starts counting out notes and change.

TAMSIN. What d'you want?

LUKE. Get me a, get me a Kronenbourg.

TAMSIN. Cool.

Don't worry, I won't spend all of it.

She goes inside.

LUKE *checks his palms for sweat and rubs them on his trousers. Then cracks his knuckles for good measure.*

He looks at the field across from the pub. Gets out his phone and takes a photo of it, and one of the sky.

TAMSIN *returns with two beers and some change. Gives* LUKE *one of the beers.*

LUKE. Thanks.

Quiet.

TAMSIN *concentrates on rearranging the change into little coin stacks, in ascending value.*

When LUKE *notices her:*

TAMSIN. You carry this much change around, you must be raking it in.

LUKE. Oh, totally, yeah.

More like –

What's less good than raking?

I've only got like a really tiny rake.

He mimes a miniature rake. TAMSIN *grins into her glass before taking a sip.*

TAMSIN. Oh god that is really nice.

Thanks.

LUKE. S'fine.

A kind of awkward, kind of peaceful pause.

TAMSIN. Maybe I should get drunk for tomorrow.

LUKE. Oh, mate, don't do it. I did a day hungover and it was shite. Would not recommend. Day felt like five times longer than normal.

TAMSIN. Really?

LUKE. Mm.

It was, the night before was when all my mates were leaving, and they were like, we've got fifteen hours on a bus, obviously we need to be proper smashed, right, so we all stayed up and kicked around near The Point till their bus came at like… 2 a.m. And then it was just me, smashed, 2 a.m., at The Point which is like a fucking graveyard now anyway, I was like… even without work tomorrow this would be depressing.

Pause.

TAMSIN. Has it been bad without your mates?

LUKE. Just fucking dry, you know?

It's okay, but. *That* during the day, just me and my *mum* in the evenings, like…

TAMSIN. Your mum's car is the one with the Jesus thing on the dashboard, right?

LUKE. Yeah.

TAMSIN. She always picks you up.

LUKE. Yeah. She does.

TAMSIN. I'd've left by now if I were you.

The warehouse I mean.

LUKE. But… Tamsin. I'm packing at ninety per cent! You don't just walk away from skills like that!!

TAMSIN. Seriously though.

Beat.

LUKE *shrugs*.

LUKE. I mean, I wouldn't be able to get anything else before I go to college, y'know?

I tried to get a paper round first, cos that's like, classic – and exercise – but. This was the only thing going.

I guess picking is exercise, though. Kinda.

TAMSIN. Kinda. Yeah.

Pause.

What're you doing at college?

LUKE. BTEC Diploma.

(*Warning her jokily.*) Don't say it!

TAMSIN. I – wasn't gonna say anything.

What's it in?

LUKE. Uniformed Public Services.

TAMSIN. What's that, like, army?

LUKE. Well, yeah, that's part of it but I'm gonna try for emergency services cos I really wanna work in an ambulance crew.

TAMSIN. Wow.

Wow. Yeah, that.

Beat.

That's so good. Good for you. I'll drink to that.

Pause.

Hang on, that's how you know all the first-aid stuff, isn't it!

LUKE. Yeah.

TAMSIN. I thought maybe you were just making it up.

LUKE. Nah! I did a Red Cross course and everything. I've got a certificate.

TAMSIN. Right.

So what did you have to get for the BTEC? Like, good Biology grades, or?

LUKE. Five Cs including English and Maths.

TAMSIN. Okay. That's not too bad.

LUKE. Ehh. I only got Maths by one mark.

TAMSIN. Maths is okay when you get down to it.

LUKE. No it's not. Don't lie to me.

TAMSIN. It is, it's sort of like a game. I was all right at Maths. And Physics. Space and star cycles and things.

LUKE. Ahh, we must have done different exam boards, I dunno any of that.

TAMSIN. White dwarfs and stuff?

LUKE *shakes his head*.

Oh, it was cool – like you know how a star before it's a star is just this big cloud of gas, right? Like made of hydrogen and stuff?

LUKE. No, but, sure.

TAMSIN. Okay, basically... so gravity means the hydrogen all kinda clumps together and it gets really really dense and really really hot, and then after a while the hydrogen's under *so* much pressure clumping together that it starts to make helium, and that makes energy, and it basically keeps going like that in a cycle for billions of years. And it's like a massive plasma fireball type thing.

LUKE. Okay.

TAMSIN. But then, hydrogen starts running out – and so then it can't make helium, so *then* it can't make energy any more, and so the, the middle of the star – the core, shrinks into like this tiny little white dwarf and all the outer layers expand and kind of... burn out and turn to dust. And the star basically dies.

LUKE. It dies?

TAMSIN. Yeah.

Beat.

LUKE. Wow.

You are such a neek.

TAMSIN. Fuck off.

LUKE. It's cool!

TAMSIN *grins*.

TAMSIN. No it's not.

LUKE. It is! I couldn't do any of that bollocks. Why aren't you going to college?

TAMSIN. I didn't have to. We were still allowed to leave at sixteen.

LUKE. Yeah – but why didn't you go anyway?

Beat.

TAMSIN *shrugs. She fiddles with one of the coins. She flips it and covers the result with her hand before looking.*

TAMSIN. Um.

My GCSEs were – kinda crap.

I think Collier really regretted letting me in, in the end.

LUKE. Why?

TAMSIN. There was just loads going on at the time. With, with my mum, mostly. I was doing all these hospital visits, so.

LUKE. Right.

You could always retake if you wanted though, like three of my friends are retaking English.

Pause.

TAMSIN. You remember what Dean was like at school? Like, a bit – a bit weird?

LUKE. Yeah.

TAMSIN. He kinda got worse.

Pause.

Like, pretty bad.

I kind of have to look after him.

LUKE. Oh.

Right.

TAMSIN. I mean it's fine. It's fine really, I'm not being like 'feel sorry for me'.

LUKE. Okay.

TAMSIN. It's just that all that stuff's kind of, y'know. Top priority.

Pause.

Yeah.

Pause.

LUKE. I don't wanna drag the mood down, like, so / if you don't wanna –

TAMSIN. No, no it's – [fine] Don't worry.

Pause.

Um. D'you reckon I can get all my vitamin D in one go out here?

LUKE....dunno, but you need it.

TAMSIN. Shh.

LUKE. No I mean it, look –

He goes to compare his forearm against TAMSIN's *and she pulls away, laughing.*

TAMSIN. Oh my god that's so not fair!

LUKE (*jokily*). Don't sweat, I'm not judging, I know you're good people.

TAMSIN. Yeah.

Pause.

She bites the bullet.

Luke.

LUKE. Mm.

TAMSIN. At – um, at school, did you ever see what Dean did?

LUKE *tries to work out what she means and shakes his head.*

Um.

Mainly it's, it's his hair.

Like – he spends hours in the loo doing – whatever – with it.

I know it's weird.

LUKE. I mean –

TAMSIN. No, it is. It is.

We – like, we used to live a bit further out, near Willen Park – this was years ago – and my mum got this letter through the door – some neighbour had posted them to everyone, warning about a boy who'd been hanging round the houses who looked 'menacing', that if we kept seeing him we should tell police. And we read the description and it – mentioned the hair.

LUKE. Oh man.

I get those looks too sometimes. If I'm out with my friends.

TAMSIN. Really?

LUKE *shrugs*.

LUKE. You can get why.

TAMSIN. But you're not –

Beat.

I dunno.

LUKE. It's crap. I know.

TAMSIN. I get why she thought that about him, though.

Cos he looks like a fucking weirdo, he comes off like the kind of person who mumbles to themselves on the street, you know?

LUKE. He can't help it though, can he?

TAMSIN. No. He can't.

But I sometimes can't stop seeing him how other people see him. Even when no one's around. And then I start wondering if he *can* help it and he just doesn't want to and I get so fucking angry and mean and I know that's shitty. But I just. I get it – obviously no one will hire him. I wouldn't. If there was something he could do I'd be like yes, brilliant, amazing. But.

Beat.

LUKE. D'you know why it got worse?

TAMSIN. I. I mean sometimes I think it's to do with our dad leaving. But then some of the things he did even before that, when he was still a kid really, so. I dunno.

Did you feel like that when your dad left?

LUKE. I mean, *I* didn't but.

My mum got proper, proper lonely. Like she didn't say anything but I knew she'd've been sad if I went to Amsterdam. And now she keeps saying she don't want me to move away after college.

TAMSIN. Right.

LUKE. And she's my mum, and we're tight, but. I really don't wanna stay just me and her at home.

TAMSIN. No.

Pause.

LUKE. Sorry, that was…

TAMSIN. Don't worry.

LUKE. I don't normally go on like that.

TAMSIN. Me either.

Pause.

LUKE. I should probably bounce.

TAMSIN *checks her watch.*

TAMSIN. Yeah. Me too.

She doesn't move.

I can't go in tomorrow.

LUKE. What, you / can't?

TAMSIN. No, I, I physically can, just.

I *can't*.

They're gonna counsel me.

LUKE. You make it sound like they're gonna shoot you or something. 'They're gonna *counsel* me!'

TAMSIN. You can laugh, you're making ninety per cent of your target.

LUKE. Oh yeah, ninety per cent of my target, I am *living the dream*.

Just don't argue with them.

TAMSIN. I know, I know. But it's like you said earlier, it's…

LUKE. Take it on the chin, think about other shit like – I dunno – star life cycles, whatever – wait for them to stop talking, and just – go with whatever they say.

TAMSIN. That's what you'd do?

LUKE. Yeah.

I mean, in a few years that whole place's gonna be run by robots anyway. Just tell 'em what they wanna hear and move on, y'know?

Pause.

TAMSIN. How do I get what *I* want though?

LUKE. Um. Like to persuade someone, you use rhetorical questions.

And facts. And emotive language.

TAMSIN grins.

TAMSIN. You wanna write a letter to the DWP for me?

LUKE. If you'll spell-check it, sure.

Beat.

TAMSIN. Don't head off yet.

LUKE. It'll get cold really soon though.

Pause.

How far away is yours?

Slightly stunned pause on TAMSIN's *part.*

TAMSIN. Like. Five minutes. That side of Century Avenue.

LUKE. Oh, sick. We can have a cup of tea or something.

TAMSIN....

LUKE. What?

TAMSIN....um, Dean'll still be up.

LUKE. Yeah?

TAMSIN. But he doesn't really – like –

LUKE. What?

Beat.

TAMSIN....Okay. Okay.

She gets up and the two leave together.

Scene Six

TAMSIN *and* LUKE *enter the flat.* DEAN *is in the bathroom, headphones in.*

TAMSIN *approaches and knocks the door gently.*

TAMSIN. Dean?

He can't hear, so she sends him a text message. He reads it and takes his headphones out.

DEAN. What?

TAMSIN. Everything okay?

DEAN. Fine.

TAMSIN. Yeah?

I've got a friend coming over, do you wanna say hi?

DEAN. Are they there?

TAMSIN. No –

She bats LUKE *away.*

– they're coming over in a few minutes.

LUKE *dutifully goes to wait outside.*

DEAN. Who is it?

TAMSIN. It's a boy from work who used to go to school with you. Luke Mburu. Not someone new.

Do you wanna come out and say hello when he arrives?

DEAN. I'm okay.

TAMSIN. Or – not right away, but you could come out when you feel ready? Before he leaves?

DEAN. How long is he staying?

TAMSIN. Dunno. Few hours I guess.

He remembers you.

Said you used to be good at history sources or something, I dunno.

DEAN *taps the tub of hair gel, psyching himself up to:*

DEAN. Okay.

He taps the tub some more.

TAMSIN. Yeah?

DEAN. Yeah.

TAMSIN. Awesome.

She begins to walk away from the door and then remembers to say:

Thanks.

TAMSIN *goes to open the door and lets* LUKE *back in. She speaks to him with her voice lowered, so* DEAN *doesn't hear.*

He's gonna come out in a moment.

Just don't – don't judge him, okay? If he does something that seems weird or his face makes weird expressions or – he can't help it. And like, don't mention people from Hartley or anything, cos it'll embarrass him –

LUKE. I know. Bruv, gimme some credit here.

TAMSIN. Sorry. I'm –

LUKE. Chill.

TAMSIN. Okay. Okay.

DEAN. Tamsin?

TAMSIN *goes into the bathroom.*

Can you…?

He indicates a small mirror on the counter.

TAMSIN. Sure.

She holds it up so DEAN *can see the back of his head, as he continues to work on his hair.*

Outside the bathroom, LUKE *looks at the Jobcentre forms on the table.*

He sees a few items of TAMSIN'*s clothing on the floor, and gingerly picks them up, looking at each one with a slight curiosity, feeling the texture. He folds them neatly over a chair.*

TAMSIN *and* DEAN *come out of the bathroom.* DEAN *is awkward throughout, but is making a lot of effort.*

DEAN. Hey.

LUKE. Hey.

Beat.

How's it going?

DEAN. Okay. It's going okay.

He reaches up to fiddle with his hair for a moment before stopping himself.

LUKE. We've just been at The Cricketers.

Beat.

DEAN. Right.

LUKE. Y'know it?

DEAN. No.

Beat.

LUKE. Me neither – I live in Conniburrow, so. Don't usually come by Oldbrook.

Beat.

DEAN. You, um. You work with Tamsin?

LUKE. Yeah. Yeah. We're master packers, aren't we?

TAMSIN. Speak for yourself.

LUKE *notices his shoes.*

LUKE. Tamsin, do you want me to take these off inside?

TAMSIN. It's fine.

LUKE. You sure? / Cos I can –

TAMSIN. Seriously, it's fine.

LUKE. Some people are – y'know. Weird about it. I'll go to someone's house and forget and then I can feel their eyes on my shoes like *arrgh…*

DEAN. It's not a big deal for us.

LUKE. Right. Okay. Sound.

Pause.

(*To* DEAN.) Hey. Do you remember how in Hartley there was all them words on the walls when you first walked in? You remember that?

DEAN. Yeah.

LUKE. What were they? Like, Commitment, Passion…

DEAN. Endeavour.

LUKE. Endeavour, yeah yeah yeah. At the warehouse – 'fulfilment centre', sorry – they've got the same thing. Not, like, the same words, but right near the door they've got like this massive slogan thing: Work. Enjoy. Improve.

Beat.

Dunno why I brought that up, it's – not really the same thing –

DEAN. It's marketing.

LUKE. Yeah. Yeah, it is. You're right.

DEAN. It's trying to make you feel like you're important.

LUKE. Yeah.

Beat.

Man, what the hell is that about, am I right though?

DEAN. Yeah. Weird.

LUKE. Yeah.

Pause.

DEAN. – I'm gonna go to bed, is that –

He looks at TAMSIN.

TAMSIN. Yeah, that's fine, you go.

Just before DEAN *has left the room,* TAMSIN *approaches him.* LUKE *may studiously look away.*

She still doesn't want to say anything in front of LUKE, *but clasps* DEAN*'s shoulder in a way that says 'well done'. He acknowledges it, but if he says anything it's too quiet to hear.*

He exits.

TAMSIN *turns back to* LUKE.

LUKE. I dunno why I said that stuff about my shoes –

TAMSIN. Nah, don't worry! Not gonna give you half a point for it or anything.

She laughs.

That was – like I don't think he's ready to, y'know, go for a pint with us or whatever, but –

I don't remember the last time he spoke to someone like that.

Just – yeah. Cheers.

LUKE. No problem.

He fist-bumps her.

Pause.

TAMSIN *notices the clothes on the chair, and snatches them up.*

TAMSIN. Sorry, place is a complete –

Smells them.

– need to go in the wash –

She puts them away hurriedly.

Sorry.

LUKE. I was gonna ask.

TAMSIN. Yeah?

LUKE. When I see a star, how do I know if it's dying?

This is really gonna distract me now.

TAMSIN. Well. You can't really see white dwarfs, they're too small.

LUKE. If you had a telescope though?

TAMSIN. It'd have to be, like, industrial level. I dunno much about it.

I'm sorry it's such a mess in here, I didn't think I'd –

LUKE. I've got a Kit Kat.

TAMSIN *is confused.* LUKE *holds up the Kit Kat, then explains:*

I just – found it in my pocket. D'you want some?

TAMSIN. *– obviously* yes. There's only one answer to that.

LUKE. Might be a bit melty though.

He breaks it in half, starts eating one stick and puts the other on the table.

I thought it was one with four sticks for a minute and got *really* excited, but this'll do for now.

TAMSIN *sits down and has a nibble of the second half.*

TAMSIN. They're really small, actually. I swear they're bigger than this.

Unless it's just *me* getting bigger.

LUKE. Nah, that's Chunkys.

TAMSIN.…actually, yeah.

Pause.

LUKE. Also… also also…

He fishes his phone out of his pocket, switches the screen on, and hands it over to TAMSIN.

Look.

TAMSIN.…I can't get in, you've got a passcode.

LUKE. Oh – sorry –

TAMSIN. You and your fancy phone!

He takes it back and fiddles around with it.

LUKE. I was looking up – when I was outside – arrgh, why won't it come up…

He gives up and discards the phone.

Look – MKC does part-time courses. So you wouldn't have to be in all day every day. And it's like just round the corner. So you wouldn't have to leave Dean for hardly any time at all.

TAMSIN. Do they give you commission to recruit people or something?

LUKE. Course, I only do warehouse work as like my passion project, yeah?

TAMSIN. Cos, y'know, if this is a pyramid scheme you have to say.

Beat.

LUKE. You'd be fine. You wouldn't have to worry about not knowing anyone, cos I'd be there. I'd hook you up.

Pause.

TAMSIN. I'd have to ask for all this special treatment. Again.

LUKE. That's okay.

TAMSIN. I ask for so much already.

Pause.

And what would I even do afterwards?

LUKE. Dunno. Don't matter.

TAMSIN. It does matter.

LUKE. No, / cos

TAMSIN. If Dean's the same as he is now I won't be able to go and do any work, so what's the point?

LUKE. I just think you'd be *good* at it. I think you'd have fun. I think there's no point *not* doing it just cos you're scared / it won't work.

TAMSIN. Oh my god –

LUKE. You know I'm right, Taz.

Beat.

You could do one year, part time. Resit your GCSEs, they have like a special course for that. And then you can stop and look after Dean, right, or you might like get an A and then you can go and do part-time A levels or a BTEC or – whatever, I dunno, what would you wanna do?

Beat.

TAMSIN. Physics. Obviously.

And maybe like.

Law or something?

LUKE. Okay. I think I've still got my booklet thing at home, I'll bring it in for you, yeah?

Beat.

TAMSIN. Yeah.

LUKE. Okay.

Pause.

TAMSIN. Jesus, I haven't drunk in ages, I think the beer went right to my head.

LUKE. Eat something. Eat the Kit Kat.

TAMSIN. Maybe I should do some yoga.

She lies face-down on the floor, and then pushes herself up on her arms.

Downward Dog.

Wait, no, Upward Dog.

LUKE. What you on about?

TAMSIN. Oh my god, my back feels so much better. Man.

She tries to transition into Downward Dog, and her socks make her slip.

Ow. Ow. Ah.

LUKE. You okay?

TAMSIN. Oh yeah, yeah. Just – better go into – Child's Pose.

After a few moments in Child's Pose – with LUKE *watching her – she lifts her head up and quickly checks her watch, before reassuming her position.*

LUKE. What time is it?

TAMSIN. Are you tired?

LUKE. No.

TAMSIN. Okay.

I'm gonna... wind this back...

Beat.

LUKE. What time is it now?

TAMSIN. Seven-thirty.

LUKE. Sick.

Beat.

Yo. Tamsinator.

Tasmania.

TAMSIN.…yeah?

LUKE. You gonna get off the floor or you gonna just stay there?

TAMSIN.…I'm gonna get off the floor.

She turns over to lie on her back.

In a moment.

Yoga's meant to be good for anxiety, right?

Yoga and smoking.

LUKE. Why you anxious?

TAMSIN. I'm not.

Pause. LUKE *joins* TAMSIN *on the floor.*

Are you going to sleep?

LUKE. I'm just closing my eyes.

Pause.

TAMSIN. Alabama… Alaska… Arizona… Arkansas…

LUKE. What you doing?

TAMSIN. Sending you to sleep.

It's a rhythm. It's calming.

LUKE. You're *so weird*, man.

TAMSIN (*protesting jokily*). I'm not!

LUKE. And I'm not tired.

TAMSIN. Yeah, I know, I know, you're just closing your eyes.

Pause.

I keep like. Thinking the post is gonna come.

LUKE.…it's night-time.

TAMSIN. Yeah I know.

Beat.

LUKE *sits up.*

LUKE. Hey.

TAMSIN. Mm?

LUKE. You know that album with the – y'know, with the motorbike on the front?

TAMSIN. *Bat Out of Hell II.*

LUKE. Yeah, yeah. What was that song you sang?

TAMSIN. I didn't sing anything.

LUKE. No you did, you sang a line from one of them.

TAMSIN. 'I Would Do Anything For Love (But I Won't Do That)'?

LUKE. Yeah! Yeah yeah yeah. I'm gonna look it up on YouTube.

He fiddles with his phone for a moment.

TAMSIN. It's like twelve minutes long.

LUKE. …ah, I'm out of data anyway.

Do me a clip of it.

TAMSIN. What?

LUKE. I'll get a beat going, you do vocals.

TAMSIN. No.

LUKE. But you said it was really good! Are you gonna leave me hanging?

TAMSIN. That's a really weird thing to ask, Luke.

LUKE. No it's not, I always do this with my friends, we're like famous for it at school. It's – it's like, a capella or whatever. It's good for you, yeah, it releases endorphins.

TAMSIN. If Dean doesn't have his headphones on it'll disturb him.

LUKE *(calls)*. Dean?

No answer.

He's fine.

TAMSIN. I mean – it's still twelve minutes long but I could –
I could give you a really condensed version.

LUKE. Sick.

TAMSIN. Um – okay.

Beat.

So I think it starts off with all these motorbike noises –

You have to imagine there's like hairspray and dry ice
everywhere. It's 1993 but still basically feels like the eighties.

And then there's the piano riff that goes like –

She imitates the piano riff.

Do you know it now?

LUKE. Gimme some bars. First verse.

TAMSIN. Okay, it starts with – um –

She hums/sings her starting note.

Just, um, making sure –

It's like –

Doing her best Meat Loaf impression, she starts to sing.

The lyrics TAMSIN *chooses can be improvised – she might
not remember all of them and substitute other words. It
should definitely feel silly. When appropriate,* LUKE *could
even join in somehow, singing or doing a drumbeat. She
should include the penultimate line about 'screwing around',
because after taking a moment to come down from the end of
the song she says:*

Cos that's what it is, apparently. A long massive denial of
cheating.

LUKE. If he takes that long to say he won't cheat on her,
doesn't that mean that / he's gonna –

TAMSIN. He's probably gonna cheat on her? Yeah, maybe.
That tends to be how it works.

Such a stupid song. Oh my god.

LUKE. I've genuinely never heard it ever in my life.

TAMSIN. I don't even know how I heard it. I had this like random CD but I dunno where it came from.

LUKE. You do a pretty sick piano riff.

TAMSIN. Ha. Thanks. Why isn't air-piano more of a thing?!

LUKE. Literally!

TAMSIN. If I had like all the time in the world I would start an eighties cover band all on air-instruments.

LUKE. I would pay to see that.

TAMSIN. No you could come for free.

LUKE. Oh yeah?

TAMSIN. Obviously!

They do a bro shake.

Their hands remain clasped for a long moment afterwards.

TAMSIN *really slowly leans in and kisses* LUKE *on the cheek – but doesn't pull away.*

He turns his head and kisses her properly.

They're both nervous.

After a moment, TAMSIN *breaks away, almost laughs.*

LUKE. What? What's funny?

TAMSIN. No, nothing.

It's okay.

It's okay.

She kisses him again.

Scene Seven

The fulfilment centre. The clock reads 17.29. TAMSIN's counter is at 370, with an average of 284.

The bell goes for the end of the day. TAMSIN stops, and notices her count.

TAMSIN. Wow.

The clock reads 17.36. The LEAD walks in briskly.

LEAD. Okay.

Pause. He catches his breath, sees her looking at the clock.

This won't take too long.

TAMSIN. I had the weirdest packages today.

LEAD. ...

TAMSIN. Like I had about five separate packages that were just bottles of gin. How weird is that? I guess cos it's Friday people are like 'Arrgh, I need a proper pick-me-up tonight.'

Beat.

LEAD. You know why we're having this meeting, right?

TAMSIN. Yep.

She realises she needs to say it.

Cos I've got two points.

LEAD. Yeah. And if you get another point we would, company policy means we would be obliged to release you from your current contract. So this is really your chance to think about your productivity, and improve it before it gets to that point.

Normally by now, after a couple of weeks, we would expect people to be making one hundred per cent of their original target, if not more.

So we need to look at why that's not happening and identify some immediate practical goals.

Can you identify any specific errors or choices that have contributed to your failure to meet standard productivity targets?

TAMSIN. Sometimes I get new cardboard cuts and that slows me down.

LEAD. Okay. Good. Can you think of any immediate practical goals that can increase your productivity in this regard?

TAMSIN. I get cuts when I rush, so.

LEAD. Well, one thing I've noticed is that when people are using the same hands to do the same things, hour on hour, they find carpal tunnel tends to set in and that increases the chance of injury. So you might want to consider changing what each hand is doing every so often.

Shall we put that down as a suggested objective?

TAMSIN. Okay.

LEAD. If you can think of something else we can put something else down.

TAMSIN. I just think changing hands would slow me down more. Cos I have to get into a rhythm to even make these numbers.

LEAD. Okay.

TAMSIN. But we can put that down.

LEAD. Sure.

He writes for a moment.

Do you consider that you possess any psychological barriers to your productivity?

TAMSIN. Sorry?

LEAD. I've got a space here if you can name any psychological barriers.

Pause.

TAMSIN. I try really hard.

LEAD. Just one line. Doesn't have to be negative.

TAMSIN. I got 370 just now.

LEAD. Do you want to do better?

TAMSIN. At the end of the day and everything.

LEAD. Tamsin. Do you want to do better?

TAMSIN....

    Yeah.

LEAD. So let's say that what you struggle with is maintaining a positive attitude to your targets.

    He writes.

    Right – only a few more – do you believe that your only limitations are the limitations you set for yourself?

TAMSIN....

    Do you want me to –

LEAD. In those words is fine.

TAMSIN. My only limitations are the limitations I set for myself.

LEAD. Okay. Right. Thanks.

    The LEAD *writes a few sentences on his clipboard.*

    Sign here –

    She does, and he sets his clipboard aside.

    Okay. Let's talk.

    Beat.

    You're with Welling, right? Your agency?

TAMSIN. Quartz.

LEAD. Right. Have they got anything else they could line up for you?

TAMSIN. Are you firing me?

LEAD. I'm just asking. Do they?

TAMSIN. No.

LEAD. You've checked?

TAMSIN. Obviously I have.

LEAD. And you're grateful, in this environment, for this job existing? And you being able to have it?

TAMSIN. ...yeah.

LEAD. Okay. So the priority is keeping it.

TAMSIN. For now. Yeah.

LEAD. Sure.

But whatever's going on for you out there, whatever people are saying to you, you have to leave it at the door.

TAMSIN. But it's – I wouldn't care if it was just hard work. That's fine, I can work hard, whatever. It's not like I think I'm too good for this cos I don't.

LEAD. Good.

TAMSIN. It's all the other stuff.

When you assume I'm gonna steal things, that makes me *want* to, cos y'know, why not, not like you're gonna trust me either way, right?

LEAD. Do you think I'm important? You really think they wouldn't fire me in a second if they had a reason?

I have to be twice as professional. I *have* to be able to say yes I timed their toilet breaks, yes I tried all of the above tactics when they were falling short on target, yes I did everything I could.

And this has never been a stopgap for me.

TAMSIN. I know.

LEAD. I've got a daughter who grows out of her clothes and school shoes every year. You know how much that costs?

TAMSIN. Yeah. That's…

LEAD. Look. There are people at the top of this. And as far as they can see, they're doing the right thing. They don't see it from this – angle, they don't see it from here, because they just get numbers in the red and they work out how to put them in the black. And it will be the same anywhere else you go.

So you have to remind yourself that no one is targeting you. None of this is personal.

TAMSIN. They wouldn't do all of this if they didn't think we'd skive off at any moment.

LEAD. Honestly? I don't think they think about you at all.

I mean – do you think about where your clothes come from? How much that child earned?

He goes back to paperwork. TAMSIN *doesn't move until he notices she's still there.*

That's it. You can go.

TAMSIN. Can I come in tomorrow?

The LEAD *makes some calculations in his head.*

LEAD. We've already covered tomorrow, I'm afraid.

Quartz should text you to confirm but I'll probably need you back 7 a.m. Sunday. Okay?

Beat.

TAMSIN. Yeah, sure.

LEAD. You can spend some time at home.

TAMSIN. Yeah.

LEAD. Is your brother disputing the decision?

TAMSIN. Sorry?

LEAD. His Fit for Work decision.

Is it getting looked at?

TAMSIN. – yeah. Yeah, we've sent off new evidence, so.

LEAD. Good luck. I'll keep my fingers crossed for him.

Beat.

TAMSIN. Thanks.

Scene Eight

TAMSIN *lights the tealight on the table, and sits down, resting her chin on her hands and fixing her gaze on the candle.*

She might put her hands together, as if in prayer – or whisper urgently to herself.

Slowly the room's light returns, but is still quite low when a decisive 'thunk' comes, loud enough that the item feels like it could have been dropped from the sky.

TAMSIN *springs awake immediately, somehow knowing what has arrived.*

She collects a large brown envelope, sets it on the kitchen table and stares at it.

She takes a deep breath and opens the envelope. Out of it come numerous documents – photocopies of sick notes, a WCA report, various letters of correspondence.

TAMSIN *sifts through all of these on the kitchen table until she finds the most recent one. She reads it.*

It's the wrong news.

TAMSIN *searches for her phone – it's somewhere underneath all the papers.*

She composes a text, sits down, and buries her head in her arms.

DEAN *emerges from his room, in his nightclothes and a hat, holding his phone.*

DEAN. Did we not get it?

> *Pause.*

> Are we gonna appeal?

> *Pause. As if she didn't hear him:*

> Are we gonna appeal?

> TAMSIN *slowly sits up.*

TAMSIN. It says we can't.

DEAN. What?

TAMSIN. At the bottom. 'You must seek a mandatory reconsideration before you can appeal a decision.'

DEAN. I thought we did. I thought this was a mandatory reconsideration.

TAMSIN. I think it's…

> There was some reason they couldn't. Hang on.

> '…your adviser's letter dated 6th August requesting a mandatory reconsideration… Before this can be undertaken, we have to *review* our decision and provide you with an explanation of our reasons…

> 'We attempted to contact you by telephone on the 19th August and did not receive an answer…

> 'This means we have been unable to proceed with a mandatory reconsideration…'

> Um…

> Ah – 'We have taken your adviser's disputes into account in our review, but it must be noted that the Health-Care Professional is considered to be impartial and medically informed…

> We accept that you have difficulties that… blah blah blah… but consider that said health conditions do not limit your

functional abilities sufficiently for work for Employment and
Support Allowance purposes'

Pause.

Look. Didn't even put a dot at the end of that, that's how
much time and effort they're putting in. Look.

DEAN. Maybe they're dyslexic.

TAMSIN. I'm not gonna make excuses for them.

I don't know what we do now. I.

Pause.

DEAN *is tapping on the table.*

When he feels TAMSIN *looking, he takes his hands away
from the table and sits on them.*

We're gonna make it without them. Okay? Fuck them. Fuck
them and their fucking review and reconsideration and all
that bollocks, I don't fucking care, we can do this ourselves,
we can – I can work, and – this – this isn't fucking *fair.*

I can't keep doing this.

I can't. I'm so fucking *tired.*

And you just –

You act like you don't even *miss her*

Pause.

DEAN. I don't wanna talk about that.

TAMSIN. No. Obviously not. Obviously you don't fucking
want to.

DEAN. It's too –

TAMSIN. What?

DEAN *tries to say something and can't find the words.*

What?! What is it?

DEAN *goes into the bathroom, and closes the door.*

He takes up one of his pots of hair gel.

He steels himself, and then throws it into the bathroom bin.

He does the same thing with his comb – his scissors – all his pots of gel – then takes the rubbish bag and goes to put it in the larger kitchen bin. Every single time he throws something away it's agony for him.

You don't have / to

DEAN. Shut up shut up I just need –

After putting the bag into the bin, he forces himself to sit down again, and sits on his hands.

He remembers something, and goes into his bedroom.

He brings out two more pots of gel, that haven't even been opened. He bins them, and then sits on his hands again.

Are you at work tomorrow?

TAMSIN. I think so.

DEAN. Oh. Okay.

After, could you help me with –

I'm going to try and stop with the, with the…

I might cut it tomorrow. So I can't do anything.

TAMSIN. Are you sure?

DEAN. Yeah.

TAMSIN. Okay, if you're – you know, if you're positive about this.

DEAN. I want to try and cut it out.

He tries to smile at his own joke.

Um.

Just make things easier. Cos I know it's all stupid. I know that.

Beat.

Is that the right thing to do?

TAMSIN. I only want you to do what you're comfortable with.

DEAN. I'm comfortable with this.

TAMSIN. On a scale of one to –

DEAN. Ten. I'm ten comfortable with it.

It'll be easier when the days get shorter.

Cos I can try and go outside more when it's dark, when it's not…

Yeah.

Beat.

Can you –

TAMSIN. What?

DEAN. Cos I know they're still there, can you – (*Gestures to mean 'take them out'.*)

TAMSIN. Okay.

She takes the bin liner out and opens the front door.

Um. It's Saturday, so.

DEAN *looks at her, not understanding.*

It's gonna get collected tomorrow.

DEAN. That's fine.

TAMSIN. You sure? Cos then they're – [gone]

DEAN. I don't want to be able to go and get them.

TAMSIN. Okay.

Last chance…?

DEAN *nods.*

TAMSIN *leaves with the bin liner.*

Scene Nine

TAMSIN *gets* DEAN *out of bed. He puts his hat on, and refuses to let her help him.*

TAMSIN. Let me.

He shakes his head, and puts on his clothes himself, tapping them all the while. It's obviously difficult and distressing for him.

Come on –

DEAN. Shut up / I'm trying to –

TAMSIN. Don't tell me to shut up.

DEAN. – just, *please*, I'm trying, okay?

Pause as he finishes.

TAMSIN. Are we gonna have a good day?

DEAN. Yep.

TAMSIN. Are you sure?

DEAN. Just gimme a bit of space.

She does.

I'm gonna have a good day.

TAMSIN. Do you feel calm?

DEAN. Yeah.

I don't want you to be late, you should go.

He is tapping in rhythms of four the whole time.

TAMSIN. Please eat something today, okay?

DEAN. I will.

TAMSIN. Even if it's not what I made you, it's fine if you just want toast or something.

DEAN. I don't / eat

TAMSIN. I know you don't eat bread, it was just, it's an example.

Can you promise me?

DEAN. What?

TAMSIN. That you'll eat something.

DEAN. I already said.

Are you gonna go?

I don't want you to be late.

TAMSIN. ... All right.

I'll get back soon as I can.

(*Getting as close to him as he will let her.*) You're okay. You can do this, yeah?

TAMSIN *exits. DEAN is left continuing to tap in these patterns of four even after she's left.*

With nothing to focus on, he begins to go into the bathroom, and then stops himself. Tries tapping the kitchen table.

He goes into the bathroom, taps the sink, and runs some water over his hands. He almost wets his hair with it a few times, but manages to stop himself, his hand stuttering.

He dries his hands, returns to the kitchen, and taps the table. Getting stuck on a loop of tapping, he then sits on his hands.

He gets a can of soup from a cupboard, empties it into a pan, and then lights the hob.

He manages to stop himself going back to the bathroom by tapping on the kitchen countertop, but eventually it becomes less effective.

Eventually he goes back to the bathroom and wets his hands again.

He forces himself to dry his hands before he can let himself put the water in his hair, and goes back into the kitchen.

*He's so distracted that without thinking he touches the pan
with his left palm and burns himself.*

*He tries not to touch it with the other hand, but the need to
complete the pattern is obvious – his hand stutters in mid-air.
He tries to physically restrain himself but it's agony.*

The lights go down the moment he burns his right palm.

Scene Ten

*The fulfilment centre. The clock reads 15.21. TAMSIN's count
is at 91, with an average of 258 per hour.*

The LEAD *approaches* TAMSIN.

LEAD. We need to have a chat.

  Stop packing, I've only got a moment and I need you to pay
  attention.

She stops.

  Don't tell anyone about this, okay?

TAMSIN….okay?

LEAD. Can you promise me that?

TAMSIN. I promise.

LEAD. It's really really important you don't say anything, this
  is jobs-on-the-line sort of stuff.

TAMSIN. I won't.

LEAD. Okay. Now – none of this is set in stone and I'm not
  making any guarantees. But – we've got a few permanent
  positions coming up. Same as what you do now, but –

  Actually, keep packing. I don't want any gaps.

She starts again.

I can't give one of them to you while you're making
seventy-per-cent target.

TAMSIN. Okay.

LEAD. You understand that, right? It'd look sketchy, and it's
not worth my job if someone decided to investigate. But
you've been here nearly three weeks – in nine weeks, if
you're still here, managing one hundred per cent target, and
not got any more points, I'll have some evidence to put in
the form and your previous points'll have dropped off, so
it'll all check out okay. And then we can put your salary up
to the permanent rate, and your hours would be contracted.

TAMSIN....

LEAD. Like I said, I can't promise anything. And you *have* to
keep your head down. But if you do.

TAMSIN. Do you get to choose?

LEAD. I can make recommendations.

TAMSIN. Okay.

Beat.

LEAD. Don't rush to thank me or anything.

TAMSIN. No no, that's –

LEAD. I mean, do you want it?

TAMSIN....

Yeah. I do.

Thank you. Genuinely.

LEAD. Sure.

Numbers up, okay?

The LEAD *exits.*

The clock reads 17.10. LUKE *comes by with a trolley of totes.*

LUKE. Yo yo yo.

TAMSIN. Hi.

TAMSIN *just keeps packing as he speaks*.

LUKE. Tried to swing by earlier but they're riding me really hard today. Worst leaving present in the world.

Wagwan?

TAMSIN. This your last day?

LUKE. Yeah.

TAMSIN. When does college start?

LUKE. Tomorrow.

TAMSIN. Wow. Wow, that's – quick.

LUKE. Yeah. Well, they're 'letting me go' anyway cos I been here twelve weeks – I was gonna say like 'Oh so you're cancelling now the free trial's ending?' but I didn't think they'd get the joke.

I found the booklet, though, my mum's gonna bring it when she picks me up.

TAMSIN....thanks.

Beat.

LUKE. You okay?

TAMSIN. Do you know what you're starting out with, have you got your, um, your timetable yet?

LUKE. It's like… leadership and teamwork and things.

TAMSIN. Cool. Awesome.

You're gonna be really busy, aren't you?

LUKE. I mean. I guess, but I'll still have / time for –

TAMSIN. Not, not in a bad way, but you will.

(*Mumbling.*) You should get on, they'll be… pissed off…

LUKE. I'm leaving tomorrow, don't make a difference if they fire me now.

TAMSIN. I'm not, though.

LUKE. Not what?

TAMSIN. Leaving.

Beat.

LUKE. You're staying on?

TAMSIN. Hopefully. Yeah.

LUKE. Seriously?

TAMSIN *can't bring herself to answer for a split second too long.*

Why? Did / the

TAMSIN. Luke. Don't. Don't do this.

LUKE. I'm just asking.

TAMSIN. Thing is. This – *this* doesn't matter.

You're gonna be fine, you really are. Don't worry about all the other crap, yeah? Tell me you're not gonna worry.

LUKE. ...okay.

TAMSIN. You're gonna be really, really, *really* good.

So, it's – it's okay. I promise.

I'm gonna – my average is already shit today, so…

She starts packaging again.

LUKE *looks at her for a while, and eventually pushes his trolley away. Once she can't hear him any more,* TAMSIN *stops for a moment and steadies her breathing.*

Trying to force herself back into her routine, she packs a few items, and then finds that her next order is a massive tub of hair gel – industrial size. The gel is the same design or brand as every single one of DEAN*'s pots.*

She looks around for a moment, as if wondering whether someone is playing a trick on her.

She begins to package the tub of gel, her hands slightly unsteady.

She's about to put it on the conveyer belt, and falters, clutching the package to her chest – but then looks at the scoreboard. Her average has dropped.

She taps it twice with her left hand and twice with her right hand, and puts it on the conveyer belt.

The clock reads 17.30. The LEAD *approaches.*

Can I go?

LEAD. I'm sorry?

TAMSIN. I know what you said, and I swear I'm gonna keep my head down. I'm gonna do better than today, I absolutely completely promise I am, I just I need to go *right now*.

LEAD....this isn't gonna happen again, all right?

TAMSIN *tries to shrug off her orange vest and boots as quickly as possible.*

Give it to me.

Breathe. Okay?

Go.

She does.

Scene Eleven

DEAN *is sitting in the bathroom, wearing his hat, and continually tapping with his fingertips.*

TAMSIN *enters, dropping her bag, and calling out immediately:*

TAMSIN. Dean?

Are you okay?

She knocks on the bathroom door – but urgently this time.

Dean??

Pause.

DEAN *slides the bolt of the door, but doesn't open it.*

TAMSIN *goes into the bathroom.*

She notices his hands.

Oh god…

They're both burned, in exactly the same place. TAMSIN *touches one of the burns for a moment –* DEAN *winces and recoils.*

Sorry – sorry.

Put them under some water.

She takes hold of his hands again, and tries to put them under the tap. He jerks back.

DEAN. No –

TAMSIN. Dean, come on. Put them under the water.

He struggles and won't let her.

Come on.

Look, okay, tap for me.

She lets go of his hands and offers her own palms as a surface for him. He taps them three times with his left hand and three times with his right.

She tries to take her hands back but he grips on to them.

Again? Okay.

He taps her palms three times with his left hand, three times with his right.

She gently takes his hands again and puts them under the cold tap.

See? Doesn't sting.

Pause.

What happened?

DEAN *shrugs*.

What happened?

DEAN. I...

Pause. She waits.

I panicked.

TAMSIN. Why?

Pause.

Cos you didn't have your gel, and all your – ?

DEAN *nods*.

How did it happen?

Pause.

What were you doing?

DEAN. Cooking.

TAMSIN. But I made you food.

DEAN. Take my mind off not being able to...

He trails off.

TAMSIN. Do your hair?

DEAN....yeah.

Pause.

TAMSIN. Both of them?

DEAN. I tried not to, but – after I did one, I.

I did try not to.

I just.

I can't find any other way [to].

TAMSIN. Do you want me to take you to A&E?

He shakes his head.

I think we should go.

He shakes his head more vigorously.

DEAN. 'm fine.

TAMSIN. I don't know how to treat this, I…

DEAN. I'm not going outside.

Pause.

TAMSIN. Do we have any cling film left?

DEAN doesn't answer, but TAMSIN goes into the kitchen and searches through the drawers until she finds a roll. She returns to the bathroom and shows DEAN.

Is this okay?

She tears off a piece.

I'm just gonna wrap it over the…

Gently, she takes DEAN's hand from under the tap, turns the tap off, and covers one burn in a layer of cling film.

DEAN. Is that what you're meant to do?

TAMSIN. Yeah. I think so. Someone told me.

Is that…?

DEAN *tests out his hand, bending it slightly. It's painful.*

Don't bend it there, just –

She takes his hand back and unbends it, before starting to wrap the other one.

I was thinking – a few days ago – it was really sunny on my way in and I like started thinking about this time when – I don't know how old we were, but it was the summer holidays – and you were sitting on the doorstep – and I was listening to that Discman we had.

So I must have been. What. Ten?

And I took my headphones off and asked what you were doing and you were memorising all the states of America. And I ended up doing it as well. And we just spent – it must have been weeks – testing each other again and again on being able to recite them. And write them down alphabetically. And we did it right before bed every single night. And Mum got completely sick of us. I don't even remember why we did it, but. It was kind of amazing.

Why the states? Why not the counties? I don't know any of the counties.

Keeping his hands straight, DEAN *taps the edge of the sink with his fingertips – four times with the left and four times with the right.*

Slowly, DEAN *walks out of the bathroom, out of the kitchen, into his room.*

TAMSIN *watches from her position on the bathroom floor.*

After a moment, DEAN *opens his door, and addresses* TAMSIN *from there.*

DEAN. Are you all right?

Long pause.

TAMSIN. Did you order some more gel?

DEAN. Yeah. I thought I should probably...

Pause.

TAMSIN. No, it's, it's fine.

DEAN. I got the cheapest one I could find.

TAMSIN. I know.

DEAN. Cos I know we can't –

TAMSIN. I know.

Good stuff.

When DEAN speaks, the words sound foreign and unfamiliar to him.

DEAN. Do you want a cup of tea?

Pause.

TAMSIN. Yeah. Thanks.

They both come into the kitchen.

Being careful and awkward, hampered by his hands, DEAN goes to put the kettle on to boil.

He gets a mug ready, and puts a teabag inside.

After pouring the water, he goes to hand it over to TAMSIN – before taking it back and putting it in the microwave.

While waiting for the microwave to count down, TAMSIN notices the tealight on the kitchen table.

She considers it for a moment, searches for some matches, and lights it.

End.

A Nick Hern Book

Wish List first published in Great Britain in 2016 as a paperback original by Nick Hern Books Limited, The Glasshouse, 49a Goldhawk Road, London W12 8QP, in association with the Royal Exchange Theatre, Manchester, and the Royal Court Theatre, London

Wish List copyright © 2016 Katherine Soper

Katherine Soper has asserted her right to be identified as the author of this work

Cover image: © Shutterstock/Surrphoto

Designed and typeset by Nick Hern Books, London
Printed in the UK by Mimeo Ltd, Huntingdon, Cambridgeshire PE29 6XX

A CIP catalogue record for this book is available from the British Library

ISBN 978 1 84842 602 3